PEACE *Instead of* WAR

PEACE *Instead of* WAR

Amicable and Win-Win Conflict Resolution Without Bloodshed

Dr. Dominion V. Judah

Peace Instead of War
Dr. Dominion V. Judah

First Edition, 2023

Publisher's Name: The Ageless Press

ISBN Hardback Edition 978-0-6458613-6-5
ISBN Paperback Edition 978-0-6458613-7-2
ISBN Ebook Edition: 978-0-6458613-8-9

Dedication

I dedicate this book to God and to all individuals, families, communities, nations and regions which have in any way been negatively affected, directly or indirectly by violent conflicts, terrorism, and wars. The purpose of this book is to prevent more of such devastations from occurring in our societies any further.

Appreciation

My sincere profound appreciation goes to everyone who has ever contributed to my life and success towards making this book a reality. I love and celebrate you all.

TABLE OF CONTENTS

INTRODUCTION

In a world often marred by conflict, violence, and the devastating consequences of war, the yearning for peace stands as a fundamental human aspiration. Throughout history, societies have experienced the horrors and destruction inflicted by armed conflicts, prompting a collective realization of the urgent need for peaceful resolutions to conflicts. As the world navigates the complexities of the 21st century, the pursuit of peace has become more crucial than ever before. This book, aims to delve into the essence of peace, its significance, and its transformative power for individuals, communities, and the world.

The concept of peace extends far beyond the mere absence of war. It encompasses harmony, stability, and a commitment to non-violence. Peace offers the fertile ground upon which societies can flourish, allowing individuals to achieve their full potential and fostering equitable and inclusive development. It cultivates empathy, cooperation, and mutual respect, fostering understanding and acceptance among diverse communities. Moreover, peace provides a platform for constructive dialogue and diplomacy, enabling the resolution of conflicts through peaceful means.

War, on the other hand, represents a stark contrast to peace. It epitomizes the breakdown of human relations, sowing seeds of destruction, suffering, and deep-seated animosity. Armed conflicts tear apart families, ravage entire regions, and inflict immeasurable pain on innocent civilians. The consequences of war reverberate long after the guns have fallen silent, leaving scars that may take generations to heal. Recognizing the devastating toll of war, societies worldwide have been compelled to seek alternatives prioritizing peaceful coexistence and cooperation.

Peacebuilding is a multifaceted endeavor, demanding concerted efforts at multiple levels. It requires the commitment of governments, international organizations, civil society, and individuals to work collaboratively toward conflict prevention, resolution, and post-conflict reconstruction. At the global level, organizations such as the United Nations (UN) play a central role in promoting peace through diplomacy, mediation, and peacekeeping operations. The UN Charter, adopted in 1945, enshrines the principle of peaceful coexistence as a fundamental tenet for international relations.

Furthermore, peace is deeply intertwined with social justice, human rights, and sustainable development. Inequality, poverty, and exclusion often serve as root causes of conflicts, fueling grievances and exacerbating societal tensions. By addressing these underlying issues and striving for equality and justice, societies can lay the foundation for lasting peace. Additionally, sustainable development initiatives that promote education, healthcare, and economic opportunities can help mitigate the conditions that give rise to conflict, empowering individuals and fostering societal resilience.

Building a culture of peace requires the active engagement of individuals, who are vital agents of change. People can promote peace in their immediate surroundings through kindness, understanding, and empathy. People can contribute to the group effort of creating a peaceful society by resolving personal issues, advocating for peaceful solutions or encouraging discussion across divides.

Moreover, education plays a crucial role in nurturing a culture of peace. By instilling values of tolerance, respect for diversity, and conflict resolution skills, education equips individuals with the tools needed to address conflicts peacefully. Education should focus on academic knowledge and developing social and emotional competencies, empathy, and critical thinking. By investing in quality education for all, societies can lay the groundwork for a more peaceful and inclusive future.

In this book, we will critically examine the amicable and win-win conflict resolution strategies that can be employed to prevent war and promote peace. We will delve into the socio-economic consequences of war, shedding light on its immense costs and long-lasting impact on societies. By exploring these topics, we hope to contribute to the ongoing discourse on peace and inspire individuals, governments, and organizations to prioritize peaceful alternatives in resolving conflicts.

The pursuit of peace represents an intrinsic and fundamental human longing. It transcends the mere absence of war and encompasses harmony, justice, and mutual respect. The consequences of war are devastating and far-reaching, underscoring the urgency of prioritizing peaceful solutions to conflicts. Peacebuilding requires concerted efforts at multiple levels involving governments, international organizations, civil society, and individuals. Together, let us embark on this journey to explore the transformative power of peace and work towards creating a world where war is no longer a viable option and peace becomes the guiding principle for humanity's progress.

CHAPTER I

THE SOCIO-ECONOMIC CONSEQUENCES OF WAR

Historical evidence unequivocally demonstrates war's profound impact, as it exacts an immense toll on humanity and imposes substantial economic and social costs. From the loss of human life to the destruction of critical infrastructure, the ramifications of war reverberate across societies, leaving lasting scars. This chapter explores the multifaceted repercussions that arise from armed conflicts. Examining the detrimental effects on human capital, labor force, government institutions, political stability, and overall uncertainty aims to deepen our understanding of the far-reaching consequences of war.

DESTRUCTION OF LIVES, INFRASTRUCTURE, AND CULTURAL HERITAGE

War is a dark chapter in human history, inflicting profound and lasting societal consequences. Beyond the battlefield, the impact of war extends to the very fabric of human existence, leaving destruction in its wake. The following are the socio-economic consequences of war, its devastating effects on lives, infrastructure, and cultural heritage:

War's Impact on Lives

War, with its unrelenting violence and destruction, has a profound and devastating impact on lives, leaving a trail of devastation in its wake. Innocent civilians, who often find themselves caught in the crossfire, bear the brunt of war's consequences. Families are torn apart, communities are shattered, and lives are forever altered.

The physical toll of war on individuals is immeasurable. The violence inflicted during armed conflicts results in many injuries, ranging from minor wounds to life-altering disabilities. The scars of war run deep, both visible and invisible, leaving survivors to grapple with the physical pain and trauma that can persist long after the fighting ceases. The loss of life is perhaps the most tragic consequence, as loved ones are torn away, leaving voids that can never be filled.

Yet, war's impact extends far beyond physical injuries and death. The psychological toll inflicted on survivors is profound and long-lasting. Witnessing or experiencing violence, losing loved ones, and enduring war's constant fear and uncertainty leave indelible scars on the human psyche. Post-traumatic stress disorder (PTSD), anxiety, depression, and other mental health disorders are prevalent among war-affected people. The psychological wounds of war can continue to haunt individuals and communities for generations, shaping their daily lives and interactions.

Rebuilding shattered lives in the aftermath of war becomes a monumental task. It demands support, compassion, and resilience from individuals, communities, and governments. Physical rehabilitation programs, healthcare services, and psychological support systems are crucial in addressing survivors' immediate needs. It is easier to regain a feeling of direction and optimism for the future when there are chances for education, skill development, and employment. In order for people to feel comfort and strength, social institutions must be rebuilt, and community cohesiveness must be promoted.

The Destruction of Infrastructure

In the aftermath of war, the destruction of infrastructure stands as a stark reminder of the devastating impact on communities and societies.

Essential facilities that form the backbone of functioning societies, such as schools, hospitals, transportation networks, and utilities, bear the brunt of conflict. Once vibrant and integral to everyday life, these critical pillars crumble under the weight of war's destruction.

The loss of schools and educational institutions disrupts access to education for children and young adults. Education is the foundation upon which societies build their future. It equips individuals with knowledge, skills, and opportunities for personal and professional growth. When schools are destroyed, learning opportunities diminish, depriving a generation of children of quality education and limiting their potential for a brighter future.

Hospitals and healthcare facilities are also severely impacted by war. These institutions are vital in providing essential medical care and saving lives. The destruction of hospitals means limited access to healthcare services, leaving communities vulnerable to preventable illnesses, injuries, and maternal and child health complications. The absence of healthcare infrastructure increases the risk of mortality and hampers post-war recovery efforts, as a healthy population is essential for rebuilding and revitalizing communities.

Transportation networks, including roads, bridges, and airports, are critical arteries that enable the movement of goods, services, and people. During the war, these lifelines of connectivity and trade become targets for destruction, severing vital supply chains and hindering economic activity. The loss of transportation infrastructure isolates communities, making it difficult for people to access healthcare, education, and employment opportunities. Additionally, it hampers the delivery of humanitarian aid and slows down post-war recovery efforts, as the movement of resources becomes arduous and costly.

Utilities such as water and electricity infrastructure, essential for daily life, are also ravaged by conflict. The interruption of water delivery systems jeopardizes the availability of clean, safe drinking water, increasing the risk of waterborne illnesses and aggravating existing health issues. The destruction of electrical grids plunges communities into darkness, affecting communication, transportation, and basic services. The absence of these utilities creates immense hardships for individuals and impedes the restoration of normalcy and progress in war-torn regions.

Rebuilding infrastructure in the aftermath of war becomes an arduous and resource-intensive endeavor. It demands significant financial investment, time, and concerted efforts from governments, international organizations, and communities. The process involves physical reconstruction and planning and implementing systems that prioritize resilience, sustainability, and inclusivity. Rebuilding infrastructure is essential for restoring the foundations of society, revitalizing economic activity, and improving the quality of life for affected communities.

The restoration of infrastructure requires comprehensive assessments, coordination, and collaboration among stakeholders. It involves the expertise of engineers, architects, and urban planners who work together to design resilient and functional structures. Additionally, it necessitates the mobilization of resources and international aid to support the reconstruction efforts, ensuring that communities can regain access to essential services, revive economic activities, and rebuild their lives.

Ultimately, infrastructure reconstruction is not just about rebuilding physical structures but also about rebuilding hope, resilience, and a sense of normalcy. It is a vital step towards post-war recovery, providing the foundation for communities to heal, thrive, and progress toward a prosperous future.

Cultural Heritage Under Siege

The destruction of cultural heritage during war represents a profound loss for specific communities and humanity as a whole. Ancient monuments, archaeological treasures, and sacred sites bear witness to centuries of history and fall victim to the ruthless destruction of armed conflicts. The eradication of cultural heritage is tantamount to erasing a part of our collective identity and memory.

The preservation of cultural heritage holds immense significance in post-war societies. It serves as a symbol of resilience, unity, and the richness of diverse cultures. Cultural heritage sites embody the legacy of past civilizations, offering insights into their achievements, beliefs, and values. The destruction of these sites fractures the connection between past and present, hindering the process of healing, reconciliation, and the formation of a cohesive national identity.

Environmental Impact

War devastates the environment, leaving long-lasting scars that persist even after the cessation of hostilities. The use of weapons and warfare tactics inflicts severe damage on ecosystems, resulting in far-reaching environmental consequences.

During the war, using explosives, artillery, and chemical weapons wreaks havoc on the natural landscape. Bombings and shelling destroy habitats, kill wildlife, and disrupt delicate ecological balance. The contamination of soil, water sources, and air with toxic substances poses serious risks to human and environmental health, often leading to long-term pollution and ecosystem degradation.

Deforestation is another environmental consequence of war. Trees are felled to serve military purposes, either for fuel, construction, or strategic clearing. This widespread deforestation further exacerbates environmental degradation, as it leads to soil erosion, loss of biodiversity, and disruptions in the water cycle. As trees are essential for carbon absorption and greenhouse gas emission reduction, their destruction also contributes to climate change.

War-torn communities face additional environmental challenges in the aftermath of conflict. The depletion of natural resources, such as water, minerals, and timber, intensifies due to increased demands during wartime. This depletion hampers post-war recovery efforts and perpetuates resource scarcity, further exacerbating social and economic hardships.

The long-term environmental impact of war has far-reaching consequences for both human and ecological systems. It hampers post-war recovery and reconstruction efforts, diverting resources and attention from urgent environmental concerns. It also exacerbates vulnerabilities to climate change and natural disasters as weakened ecosystems struggle to cope with environmental stresses.

The path to recovery from war's devastation is challenging and complex. Rebuilding shattered lives, infrastructure, and cultural heritage demands a holistic approach. It requires collective efforts to address affected communities' physical, psychological, and economic needs. Investing in education, healthcare, and livelihood opportunities is essential to restore hope and stability. Preserving cultural heritage fosters a sense of identity and paves the way for healing and reconciliation. Above all, promoting peace and preventing future conflicts becomes a shared responsibility, ensuring a brighter and more harmonious future for future generations.

The socio-economic consequences of war are profound and far-reaching. The toll on lives, infrastructure, and cultural heritage highlights the urgent need for peace and conflict resolution. By understanding the devastating impact of war, we are compelled to seek alternative paths that prioritize preserving life, rebuilding infrastructure, and safeguarding cultural heritage. Through collective efforts, compassion, and resilience, we can strive to heal the wounds of war and forge a future where the devastating consequences of armed conflict are replaced with lasting peace and prosperity.

DISPLACEMENT AND REFUGEE CRISES

War inflicts profound and enduring consequences that extend beyond the immediate combat zone. Among the most devastating impacts of armed conflict are the displacement of individuals and the subsequent emergence of refugee crises. Forced migration due to war tears apart communities, disrupts social structures and causes immense human suffering. Understanding the magnitude of these crises is crucial for striving towards effective solutions, supporting humanitarian efforts, and advocating for the rights and well-being of displaced populations.

Displacement occurs when individuals and communities are forcefully uprooted from their homes and habitual places of residence as a result of conflict, violence, or persecution. This includes internal displacement within a country's borders and cross-border displacement, where individuals seek refuge in neighboring countries or beyond, forming refugee populations.

War's causes and dynamics are complex, varying across conflicts. Root causes include armed conflict, political instability, persecution, ethnic or religious tensions, and human rights abuses. The actions of armed actors, power imbalances, and strategic objectives further shape the dynamics of displacement. Parties involved in war may employ displacement as a deliberate tactic to weaken opposition, control territory, or exploit resources. Civilians often become targets of violence, resulting in forced displacement to survive.

Displacement presents significant humanitarian challenges that necessitate immediate and comprehensive responses. Displaced individuals face urgent needs, such as shelter, clean water, food, healthcare, and protection from violence and exploitation. Providing humanitarian assistance in conflict zones is extremely challenging due to insecurity, limited access, and resource constraints. Women, children, and marginalized groups are particularly vulnerable to physical and sexual violence, exploitation, and human trafficking. The breakdown of social structures and support networks exacerbates these vulnerabilities, leaving individuals without adequate protection. Protracted displacement further complicates finding durable solutions.

International law is crucial in protecting and assisting refugees and displaced populations. The 1951 Refugee Convention, along with its 1967 Protocol, establishes the rights and responsibilities of states concerning refugees, encompassing the principle of non-refoulement.

The United Nations High Commissioner for Refugees (UNHCR) works with governments, NGOs, and stakeholders to uphold the rights and well-being of refugees, seeking durable solutions through voluntary repatriation, local integration, and resettlement.

Managing displacement is a complex task that requires cooperation between governments, humanitarian organizations, and stakeholders. Challenges include:

- Ensuring the safety and security of displaced populations.
- Providing access to essential services.
- Addressing psychosocial needs.
- Finding durable solutions for long-term displacement.

Humanitarian organizations establish camps or settlements, provide emergency aid, and deliver essential services like healthcare, education, and clean water. Adequate funding, logistics, and coordination are crucial for meeting immediate needs. Long-term solutions involve promoting peace and stability, addressing root causes, and supporting post-conflict reconstruction and development. Efforts should focus on peacebuilding, conflict resolution, and socio-economic equality to prevent future displacement and promote self-reliance.

Supporting displaced populations goes beyond immediate needs, encompassing rights, empowerment, and integration. Access to quality education offers hope and a sense of normalcy for displaced children and youth, promoting socialization and a pathway to a better future. Healthcare services, including mental health support, address displaced populations' physical and psychosocial well-being. Promoting social and economic integration is vital for long-term stability and self-reliance. Inclusive policies, employment opportunities, and social cohesion efforts between displaced and host communities foster understanding, tolerance, and mutual respect.

Addressing displacement and refugee crises necessitates a coordinated international response. Governments, intergovernmental organizations, NGOs, and civil society support affected populations, advocate for their rights, and find durable solutions. International cooperation provides financial resources, technical expertise, and political support to countries hosting large numbers of displaced populations. Advocacy efforts generate empathy, mobilize support, and combat xenophobia and discrimination. The international community's commitment is essential for protecting and promoting the rights and well-being of displaced populations.

Displacement and refugee crises resulting from war inflict severe and lasting consequences on individuals, communities, and societies. Forced migration disrupts lives, creates vulnerabilities, and necessitates effective responses from the international community. Understanding the causes, challenges, and potential solutions surrounding displacement is crucial for promoting peace, supporting humanitarian efforts, and ensuring the rights and well-being of displaced populations.

ECONOMIC SETBACKS AND LONG-TERM IMPLICATIONS

War has profound and far-reaching consequences that extend beyond human suffering and destruction. One of the most significant impacts of armed conflict is its severe economic setbacks on societies. The destructive nature of war disrupts economies, undermines development efforts, and imposes long-term implications that hinder progress and stability. By understanding the magnitude of these setbacks, we can strive for effective strategies to mitigate their impact, promote economic recovery, and pave the way for sustainable development.

Disruption of Trade and Commerce

War's impact on trade and commerce has far-reaching consequences for economies and societies. Conflict zones become highly volatile and insecure, creating significant obstacles to transporting goods and conducting business operations. The disruption of trade routes, closure of borders, and severing of supply chains disrupt domestic and international trade, leading to substantial economic setbacks.

In war zones, the high levels of violence and insecurity create an environment that is unfavorable for conducting business. Companies face numerous challenges in transporting goods, including risks to the safety of their employees, damage to infrastructure, and the threat of looting or extortion. As a result, many businesses are forced to suspend or drastically scale back their operations, leading to a decline in production and trade volumes.

The closure of borders further exacerbates the disruption of trade. Governments often impose restrictions on the movement of goods and people in conflict-affected areas as a security measure. This limits the flow of goods across borders, cutting off access to vital markets and interrupting supply chains. The inability to export goods or import necessary inputs hampers the productivity and competitiveness of businesses, affecting their profitability and long-term viability.

The loss of commercial connections and market access has an economic cascade. Industries that depend largely on imports or exports are especially susceptible to interruptions brought on by conflict.

Export-oriented sectors such as manufacturing, agriculture, and mining experience a significant decline in product demand, resulting in job losses and reduced incomes. Small and medium-sized enterprises (SMEs), which often form the backbone of many economies, are especially vulnerable as they lack the resources and resilience to withstand such shocks. These businesses may struggle to access credit, face supply chain disruptions, and experience difficulty in adapting to changing market conditions.

The decline in trade has broader implications for the overall economy. Reduced trade volumes lead to lower government tax revenues, limiting their capacity to fund essential public services and invest in infrastructure development. The decline in economic activity also impacts the employment market, exacerbating unemployment rates and increasing poverty levels. As job opportunities dwindle, households face income losses, struggle to meet basic needs and experience a decline in their overall standard of living.

Furthermore, the disruption of trade can have long-term implications for the economic development of a country. Trade relationships and market access that took years to establish can be irreparably damaged during the conflict. The loss of trade partners and the deterioration of business networks make it challenging for countries to recover and rebuild their economies after the conflict ends. Rebuilding these relationships and regaining market access requires significant time, effort, and resources.

Economic Decline and Macroeconomic Instability

War inflicts a severe blow to the economy, characterized by a sharp decline in economic activity, contraction of GDP, and an overall shrinking of the economy. The destruction of infrastructure, disruption of trade, and loss of productive capacities all contribute to this economic decline, setting the stage for macroeconomic instability in war-affected countries.

The destruction of infrastructure is a hallmark consequence of war that profoundly impacts economic performance. Critical assets such as roads, bridges, power plants, and factories are reduced to ruins, impeding the functioning of industries and hindering productivity. The loss of infrastructure disrupts supply chains, impedes the movement of goods and services, and paralyzes essential sectors of the economy. This disruption cascades through the entire economic system, leading to a contraction in economic output and a decline in GDP.

The disruption of trade further compounds the economic decline. As discussed earlier, war leads to closing borders, cutting off market access, and severing trade relationships. The resulting decline in exports and imports directly affects the performance of industries heavily reliant on international trade. Reduced trade volumes lead to decreased revenue, job losses, and decreased economic activity, contributing to the overall economic decline.

The loss of productive capacities exacerbates the economic downturn caused by war. Productive assets, such as factories, machinery, and agricultural land, are destroyed or left in disrepair, severely hampering production capabilities. The decline in productive capacities stifles economic growth and makes it challenging for businesses to recover and rebuild. It also results in a scarcity of goods and services, limiting the availability of essential commodities and driving up prices.

Macroeconomic instability emerges as a significant challenge in war-affected countries. Inflation rates skyrocket as the supply of goods and services is disrupted. The scarcity of goods, combined with increased demand, leads to price volatility, eroding the purchasing power of individuals and exacerbating the hardship faced by the population. Inflation spiraling out of control makes it challenging for people and businesses to plan and invest in the economy.

Governments in war-affected countries face substantial revenue shortfalls due to the decline in economic activities. The destruction of infrastructure, disruption of trade, and loss of productive capacities diminish tax revenues and create fiscal imbalances. This limits the government's ability to fund essential services, invest in long-term development projects, and provide social safety nets to support the population. The lack of fiscal resources further exacerbates the economic decline and amplifies the challenges individuals and businesses face.

The macroeconomic instability and economic decline from war undermine investor confidence and deter foreign direct investment (FDI). Investors are reluctant to commit resources to countries experiencing conflict due to the perceived risks and uncertainties. The instability and unpredictability of the economic environment make it difficult to attract capital inflows and private investments, hindering economic growth and development. The absence of FDI limits job creation, technological advancements, and overall economic recovery.

Human Capital Loss and Labor Market Challenges

War inflicts a heavy toll on human capital, leaving lasting scars on the labor market and impeding economic development. The loss of skilled professionals, entrepreneurs, and productive workers due to death, injury, or displacement creates a significant void in the labor force, hindering economic progress.

The loss of human capital from war is a profound setback for societies. Skilled professionals, including doctors, engineers, teachers, and other specialized workers, are often among the casualties of conflict. Their expertise and knowledge, built through years of education and experience, are irreplaceable. This loss deprives individuals and their families of their loved ones and deprives the country of valuable human resources needed for development.

Displacement exacerbates the challenges faced by individuals in accessing employment opportunities. Displaced populations often struggle to find work in their host communities due to various factors, including language barriers, discrimination, and limited job opportunities. Displaced individuals may face difficulties recognizing their skills, and their qualifications may not align with the requirements of the host country's labor market. As a result, many displaced individuals find themselves in vulnerable employment, with low wages and limited job security.

Furthermore, the loss of income and livelihood opportunities experienced by displaced populations has a ripple effect on the broader economy. Reduced consumer spending and decreased purchasing powers dampen economic activity, affecting businesses and markets. The absence of productive workers and entrepreneurs hampers innovation, productivity, and economic growth. The labor market becomes less dynamic, hindering job creation and exacerbating unemployment rates.

The disruption of education systems during conflict compounds the loss of human capital. Schools and educational institutions are often targeted or used for military purposes, leading to the closure of educational facilities and the displacement of students and teachers.

Limited access to quality education hampers human capital formation and skill development, affecting the long-term prospects of individuals and the country's overall development. Children and youth unable to receive a proper education face challenges in acquiring the skills and knowledge necessary for employment and economic advancement.

The loss of human capital from war has long-term economic recovery and development implications. The absence of skilled professionals and a diminished labor force hinder the rebuilding of infrastructure, reconstruction efforts, and the implementation of development projects. The restoration of vital services, such as healthcare and education, is delayed by a shortage of human resources with specialized knowledge and skills, further obstructing socio-economic development.

Escalating Poverty and Inequality

War exacerbates poverty and exacerbates social inequities. Economic decline, job loss, and infrastructure collapse disproportionately affect vulnerable people such as women, children, and disadvantaged communities. Poverty escalation promotes a cycle of deprivation and prevents people from obtaining needs such as food, housing, healthcare, and education.

Inequality also deepens as the economic burden of war falls disproportionately on the marginalized and disadvantaged. Wealth disparities widen, and social cohesion weakens, fueling social tensions and hindering post-war reconciliation efforts. Addressing poverty and inequality becomes a critical challenge in the aftermath of war, requiring inclusive policies and targeted interventions to uplift the most vulnerable.

Debt and Fiscal Challenges

War often leads to increased public debt and fiscal challenges for affected countries. The costs of waging war, financing military operations, and reconstruction efforts strain government budgets, often resulting in large budget deficits and increased borrowing. Governments may resort to borrowing to fund immediate humanitarian needs and the costs of rebuilding infrastructure.

High debt and fiscal imbalances can impede economic recovery and development prospects. Debt servicing obligations limit the availability of funds for essential services, social programs, and investment in productive sectors. The debt burden can persist for generations, hindering future economic growth and exacerbating the long-term implications of war.

Social Disruptions and Lost Opportunities

War disrupts social structures, undermines social cohesion, and creates a lost generation of opportunities. Displaced populations face significant challenges in accessing education, healthcare, and basic services, compromising their prospects. Children and youth are particularly affected, with disrupted education leading to a lack of skills and limited job prospects.

The breakdown of social institutions and trust further hampers economic recovery. Rebuilding social cohesion and fostering inclusive societies become crucial for creating an environment conducive to economic growth and development. Investing in education, skills training, and social support programs can help mitigate the long-term consequences of war and empower individuals and communities to rebuild their lives.

Impeding Sustainable Development

The economic setbacks caused by war pose significant obstacles to achieving sustainable development goals. Sustainable development requires a stable and resilient economy, social inclusion, and environmental sustainability. The destruction of infrastructure, disruption of trade, and loss of productive capacities hinder progress toward these goals.

Rebuilding and recovery efforts need to be aligned with sustainable development principles. This involves integrating economic, social, and environmental dimensions into post-war reconstruction and development plans. By promoting inclusive and sustainable development, war-affected countries can overcome the long-term implications of conflict and create a pathway toward resilience and prosperity.

The economic setbacks resulting from war are profound and have long-term implications for societies, businesses, infrastructure, and future prospects. The destruction of infrastructure, disruption of trade, loss of human capital, and macroeconomic instability hinder economic recovery and impede sustainable development efforts. Addressing these challenges requires comprehensive strategies focusing on rebuilding infrastructure, fostering inclusive growth, promoting human capital development, reducing inequalities, and ensuring fiscal sustainability.

PSYCHOLOGICAL AND EMOTIONAL TRAUMA ON INDIVIDUALS AND COMMUNITIES

War, with its brutality and violence, inflicts physical wounds and profound psychological and emotional trauma on individuals and communities. The psychological impact of war extends far beyond the battlefield, leaving invisible scars that can last a lifetime. War trauma is a deeply personal and pervasive experience that can have a lasting impact on individuals. Many people, who have been directly exposed to war, whether as combatants or civilians caught in the crossfire, develop symptoms of post-traumatic stress disorder (PTSD). Intrusive memories, nightmares, flashbacks, and a constant state of hyperarousal become part of their daily lives. These symptoms can disrupt their ability to function, maintain relationships, and find meaning and joy in life.

Beyond PTSD, depression and anxiety often co-occur with war trauma. A sense of hopelessness, despair, and a lack of interest in once-enjoyed activities might result from the weight of the experiences that have been observed or undergone. Aside from trouble concentrating, other symptoms of emotional discomfort include disturbed sleep.

The impact of war trauma extends beyond the individual, affecting families and communities. Family members of individuals directly affected by war trauma can experience their form of secondary traumatization. As they see their loved ones go through pain, they could battle with feelings of helplessness, remorse, and despair. Family relationships can deteriorate, communication can break down, and the regular operation of the family might be interfered with.

At the community level, war's psychological and emotional trauma reverberates through social structures and support systems. The shared experiences of violence and loss can fracture communities, eroding trust and social cohesion. Divisions may emerge along ethnic, religious, or political lines, further deepening the wounds inflicted by war. Disrupted social networks and the loss of community resources such as schools, healthcare facilities, and social support services further exacerbate the challenges individuals and families face.

The inter-generational effects of war trauma are another significant aspect to consider. Survivors of war trauma may struggle with parenting, as the residual effects of their own trauma impact their ability to provide emotional support and nurture their children effectively. Children growing up in such environments may witness or experience violence, instability, and a lack of safety, which can have profound and long-lasting effects on their development and well-being. The cycle of trauma is perpetuated as the wounds of war are passed from one generation to the next.

However, amid the darkness of war trauma, there is also resilience. Individuals and communities demonstrate remarkable strength and the capacity to heal. Coping mechanisms vary among individuals, with some finding solace in social support networks, religious or spiritual beliefs, or engaging in creative outlets such as art, music, or storytelling. These coping strategies provide a sense of connection, purpose, and hope.

Promoting mental health support and healing is essential for addressing war's psychological and emotional trauma. This requires comprehensive systems that are accessible, culturally sensitive, and trauma-informed. Creating a supportive atmosphere increases mental health awareness, lessens stigma, and educates and trains community leaders and healthcare professionals.

People can process and heal from traumatic experiences using evidence-based therapies, including cognitive-behavioral therapy (CBT) and eye movement desensitization and reprocessing (EMDR). Establishing safe environments where people may express their experiences, participate in peer support, and obtain mental health assistance is critical.

Integrated care models that combine mental health support with other essential services, such as healthcare and social support, ensure a holistic approach to healing.

International organizations, governments, and local communities must collaborate to establish and strengthen mental health services in post-war settings. This includes training and supporting local healthcare providers, integrating mental health into primary healthcare systems, and establishing specialized services for trauma survivors. Research funding can also aid in a better understanding of the long-term impacts of battle trauma and help guide efficient therapies.

War's psychological and emotional trauma leaves indelible scars on individuals, families, and communities. Understanding the nature and impact of this trauma is crucial for promoting mental health support, healing, and resilience. By addressing the psychological and emotional needs of those affected by war, we can work towards building stronger, more compassionate societies that prioritize the well-being and recovery of individuals and communities torn apart by conflict.

CHAPTER 2

AVOIDING WAR: STRATEGIES AND APPROACHES

In a world that has borne witness to the devastating consequences of war, the imperative to pursue peace and seek strategies to avoid conflicts has become increasingly urgent. Throughout history, humanity has grappled with war's destructive nature and long yearned for alternatives to resolve disputes without resorting to violence. This chapter sets the stage for an exploration of the fundamental principles and practical approaches that can guide individuals, communities, and nations in their collective endeavor to steer clear of war.

The collective consciousness of humanity has been deeply ingrained with the desire to prevent and avoid war. The haunting memories of past conflicts, the immeasurable loss of lives, the shattered communities, and the enduring scars on nations have served as poignant reminders of the need to prioritize peace. From the devastation of World Wars to regional conflicts that have claimed countless lives, the consequences of war have left indelible marks on our shared history.

Let us journey to essential strategies and principles to guide us toward a more peaceful world. Understanding the root causes of conflicts is a crucial starting point. By analyzing the intricate web of factors contributing to tensions and hostilities between nations and communities, we can gain insights into the underlying dynamics that often fuel the outbreak of violence. Economic disparities, ideological differences, territorial disputes, religious or ethnic tensions, and competition over resources are just a few examples of the complex interplay that can give rise to conflicts.

DIPLOMATIC NEGOTIATIONS: TOOLS AND TECHNIQUES FOR PEACEFUL DIALOGUE

Diplomatic negotiations play a critical role in fostering peaceful dialogue and providing a framework for resolving conflicts and achieving mutually beneficial agreements. As an essential component of international relations, diplomatic negotiations are the backbone of diplomacy, guiding nations, organizations, and individuals in finding common ground and navigating complex disputes. Through diplomatic negotiations, parties can address their differences, explore compromises, and work towards sustainable solutions that promote peace, stability, and cooperation.

The Dynamics of Diplomatic Negotiations

Diplomatic negotiations are complex processes influenced by a myriad of factors and dynamics. Successful negotiators possess a deep understanding of these dynamics, enabling them to navigate the negotiation landscape effectively. To comprehend the negotiation dynamics, diplomats and negotiators must thoroughly analyze various elements.

Historical contexts provide insights into past interactions, conflicts, and agreements, shaping the perceptions and expectations of the parties involved. Cultural nuances, such as communication styles, social norms, and values, significantly impact how negotiations unfold. Being aware of these cultural intricacies helps negotiators establish rapport and build trust. Political landscapes are vital, as national interests, domestic politics, and power dynamics shape negotiation strategies. Recognizing power imbalances and disparities in influence allows negotiators to devise approaches that address asymmetries and promote fairness.

Economic factors influence negotiation dynamics, including trade relations, resources, and financial considerations. Understanding all parties' economic interests and constraints allows negotiators to propose mutually beneficial solutions. Identifying potential sources of conflict is crucial for effective negotiation strategies. By anticipating contentious issues or diverging interests, negotiators can devise strategies to mitigate conflicts and seek areas of common ground.

A deep understanding of the dynamics in diplomatic negotiations empowers negotiators to approach negotiations with clarity, insight, and strategic acumen, increasing the likelihood of successful outcomes.

Creating the Foundation: Trust and Relationship Building

Building trust is vital in diplomatic negotiations, setting the tone for constructive and collaborative dialogue. Trust is built through credibility, reliability, and shared purpose among the parties involved.

Consistent and open communication is a key element in building trust. By maintaining transparent and frequent communication, negotiators demonstrate their commitment to sharing information and fostering a climate of honesty. This helps alleviate suspicions and misunderstandings, fostering an environment of trust and cooperation.

Transparency in negotiations is crucial. When negotiators are transparent about their objectives, concerns, and limitations, it promotes an atmosphere of sincerity and builds confidence among the parties involved. Transparent negotiations also help prevent misperceptions or hidden agendas, enabling a more focused and productive negotiation process.

Developing personal connections and engaging in cultural exchanges also play a significant role in trust-building. Negotiators can establish empathy and foster mutual respect by taking the time to understand each other's backgrounds, values, and perspectives. This cultural exchange helps bridge gaps, reduces potential biases, and enhances understanding, leading to greater trust among negotiators.

Finding common ground is another essential element in trust-building. Identifying shared interests, values, or goals allows negotiators to establish a sense of collaboration and cooperation. Recognizing areas of agreement helps build rapport and creates a solid foundation for moving forward in the negotiation process.

Overall, trust and relationship building are essential components of successful diplomatic negotiations. By focusing on transparent communication, fostering personal connections, and finding common ground, negotiators can establish an environment of trust that promotes effective and constructive dialogue, increasing the likelihood of reaching mutually beneficial outcomes.

Effective Communication: The Key to Dialogue

Effective communication is crucial to diplomatic discussions because it helps parties to overcome obstacles, enhance mutual understanding, and encourage productive discourse.

Skilled negotiators understand the importance of clear and concise communication in conveying messages accurately and avoiding misunderstandings.

Active listening is a critical component of effective communication. By attentively listening to the other parties' concerns, perspectives, and interests, negotiators demonstrate respect and show a genuine willingness to understand their viewpoints. This active engagement helps build trust, encourages open dialogue, and creates an environment conducive to finding common ground.

The use of diplomatic language is essential in diplomatic negotiations. Diplomats and negotiators often employ tact, discretion, and careful wording to convey messages effectively while maintaining a respectful and non-confrontational tone. Diplomatic language facilitates the exploration of sensitive issues and reduces the likelihood of escalating tensions or provoking conflicts.

Managing emotions is a crucial aspect of effective communication in diplomatic negotiations. Negotiators must navigate potential conflicts and tensions while maintaining composure and professionalism. Negotiators can address emotional dynamics and promote productive dialogue by fostering an atmosphere of respect, empathy, and cultural sensitivity.

Effective communication in diplomatic negotiations requires active listening, attention to non-verbal cues, the use of diplomatic language, and emotional intelligence. By prioritizing clear and concise communication, negotiators can foster mutual understanding and respect, paving the way for finding mutually acceptable solutions and achieving successful outcomes.

Strategic Approaches: Balancing Interests and Compromises

Negotiators must employ strategic approaches to balance competing interests and reach compromises. One such approach is principled negotiation, also known as interest-based negotiation. This method focuses on identifying the underlying interests and needs of all parties' involved rather than fixed positions. By understanding the underlying motivations, negotiators can explore creative solutions that address the concerns of all parties. Win-win outcomes become the goal, where all parties can achieve their objectives while maintaining the integrity of the negotiation process.

Negotiation Strategies

- Collaborative, Competitive, and Cooperative
  Negotiators employ various strategies in diplomatic negotiations to advance their interests and achieve desired outcomes. These strategies can be broadly categorized as collaborative, competitive, or cooperative, each with its characteristics and implications for the negotiation process.

Collaborative strategies prioritize cooperation and the pursuit of shared interests. Negotiators employing this approach focus on building relationships, fostering trust, and finding common ground. They collaborate to find solutions to problems, actively looking for ones that fulfill the needs of all parties.

Collaborative strategies aim to create long-term partnerships and promote ongoing cooperation beyond the immediate negotiation. This approach is particularly effective in situations with mutual benefit and shared goals, allowing negotiators to leverage the strengths and resources of all parties involved.

On the other hand, competitive strategies may be employed when interests directly conflict. Negotiators adopting a competitive stance prioritize advancing their interests and asserting their positions. They may employ tactics such as asserting power, making threats, or using aggressive bargaining tactics to gain advantages over the other party. While competitive strategies can be effective in situations with limited room for compromise, they also risk escalating tensions and undermining the negotiation process. The adversarial nature of competition can strain relationships and make it challenging to find mutually acceptable solutions.

Cooperative strategies strike a balance between collaboration and competition. Negotiators utilizing a cooperative approach engage in cooperative bargaining, aiming to maximize joint gains while protecting their interests. They recognize that negotiation involves a give-and-take process, where concessions may be necessary to reach a satisfactory outcome. This approach emphasizes building relationships, fostering trust, and creating a positive negotiating environment. Cooperative strategies can help maintain a constructive atmosphere, increase the likelihood of reaching mutually acceptable solutions, and preserve ongoing relationships between parties.

The negotiation's nature, the goals and interests of the people involved, and the particular dynamics of the scenario are only a few of the variables that influence the choice of strategy. Skilled negotiators carefully assess the circumstances and adapt their strategies accordingly. Depending on the evolving dynamics and the specific issues at hand, they may employ a mix of collaborative, competitive, and cooperative approaches throughout the negotiation process.

Ultimately, the success of negotiation often lies in finding a balance between cooperation and competition. While collaborative strategies promote relationship-building and long-term cooperation, competitive strategies may be necessary to assert interests and protect vital concerns in certain situations. Cooperative strategies allow negotiators to navigate the complexities of negotiation by seeking joint gains while safeguarding their interests. By understanding the nuances of these strategies, negotiators can effectively navigate the negotiation process and work towards achieving successful outcomes that satisfy the interests of all parties involved.

Overcoming Challenges: Emotions, Deadlocks, and Impasses

In the realm of diplomatic negotiations, challenges are inevitable and can significantly impact the progress and outcome of the process. Emotions, deadlocks, and impasses are common obstacles that negotiators must skillfully navigate to ensure productive and successful negotiations.

Emotions can often run high during negotiations, fueled by the intensity of the issues being discussed and the stakes involved. Skilled negotiators understand the importance of managing emotions effectively to maintain a constructive atmosphere. Active listening, the ability to understand and validate the emotions of all parties involved, is a crucial skill in defusing tensions and promoting open dialogue. Empathy allows negotiators to put themselves in the shoes of others, fostering understanding and reducing the likelihood of emotional conflicts. Reframing, restating, or rephrasing statements to promote understanding and common ground can help mitigate emotional barriers and facilitate negotiation progress.

Deadlocks and impasses can arise when parties reach an impasse, unable to find a mutually acceptable solution to a particular issue. Skilled negotiators employ various strategies to overcome these challenges and move forward. Exploring alternative options or creative solutions can help break through deadlocks by shifting the focus from entrenched positions to a more flexible and collaborative mindset. Brainstorming sessions, where all parties are encouraged to generate and share ideas, can spark innovation and reveal potential avenues for resolution. Taking breaks or adjourning the negotiation temporarily can also provide space for reflection and reevaluation, allowing negotiators to return with fresh perspectives and renewed energy.

Flexibility is a crucial mindset in overcoming challenges in diplomatic negotiations. Recognizing that negotiations are dynamic and evolving, negotiators must be open to adjusting their positions, exploring new possibilities, and compromising when necessary. By employing creativity in problem-solving, negotiators can explore innovative solutions that consider the interests and concerns of all parties involved, enabling them to think outside the box and reach mutually beneficial agreements.

Additionally, maintaining a commitment to the negotiation process is essential, even in the face of challenges. This commitment signals a willingness to engage in constructive dialogue and an understanding that perseverance and tenacity often achieve progress.

Skilled negotiators can navigate challenges and overcome deadlocks and impasses in diplomatic negotiations by effectively managing emotions, exploring alternative options, and maintaining flexibility and commitment. These strategies foster a productive and constructive environment, paving the way for successful outcomes that satisfy the interests of all parties involved. Ultimately, the ability to overcome challenges demonstrates the resilience and skill of negotiators in reaching mutually beneficial agreements and promoting peaceful resolutions.

Sustainable Agreements and Implementation

Reaching an agreement in diplomatic negotiations marks an important milestone, but it is only the first step toward achieving sustainable outcomes. For agreements to have a lasting impact negotiators must focus on effective implementation and monitoring, ensuring that commitments are upheld, and progress is made toward the agreed-upon objectives.

Implementation of agreements requires careful planning and coordination. Negotiators must develop clear action plans and allocate resources to support implementation. This may involve establishing timelines, defining roles and responsibilities, and mobilizing the necessary financial, technical, and human resources. Adequate communication and coordination among relevant stakeholders are crucial to ensure a smooth and effective implementation.

Monitoring and evaluation mechanisms play a vital role in assessing the progress and effectiveness of implemented agreements. Regular evaluations allow for an objective assessment of the extent to which agreed-upon actions are carried out and whether they produce the desired outcomes. This feedback loop provides opportunities to identify challenges, make necessary adjustments, and reinforce successful strategies. Monitoring also helps build trust among parties by demonstrating commitment and accountability.

To ensure the longevity of agreements, it is essential to have mechanisms to address disputes or disagreements that may arise during implementation. This may involve establishing dispute resolution mechanisms, such as mediation or arbitration, to facilitate dialogue and find mutually acceptable solutions. International institutions and legal frameworks can also support enforcing agreements and resolving conflicts.

The involvement of international organizations, such as the United Nations or regional bodies, can enhance the implementation and enforcement of agreements. These institutions can provide technical expertise, and financial support, facilitating cooperation among parties. They can also play a role in mediating disputes and facilitating compliance with international norms and standards.

Regular evaluations and assessments are necessary to ensure the adaptability and effectiveness of agreements over time. As circumstances change, reviewing and adjusting agreements to address emerging challenges and incorporate new knowledge and best practices is important. This iterative process allows for continuous improvement and ensures that agreements remain relevant and responsive to evolving needs.

Diplomatic negotiations serve as the foundation for peaceful dialogue and conflict resolution. Diplomats and negotiators navigate complex international disputes by understanding the dynamics of negotiations, building trust and relationships, employing effective communication, and employing strategic approaches. By mastering the art of diplomatic negotiations, we can create a world where conflicts are resolved through dialogue, compromise, and mutual understanding. Ultimately, the tools and techniques discussed in this exploration provide valuable insights into the art and science of diplomatic negotiations, contributing to a more peaceful and harmonious global community.

MEDIATION AND THIRD-PARTY INTERVENTION

In a world often marred by conflicts and tensions, the strategic use of mediation and third-party intervention has emerged as a vital tool for preventing and avoiding the outbreak of war. These approaches offer a means to peacefully resolve disputes, facilitate dialogue, and foster reconciliation among conflicting parties.

In mediation, an unbiased third party intervenes to facilitate negotiations and assists disputing parties in reaching a mutually acceptable agreement. The mediator, often selected for their impartiality and expertise in conflict resolution, assists in clarifying issues, managing communication, and exploring potential solutions. Mediation offers a non-coercive and voluntary process that empowers the disputing parties to take ownership of the resolution and find common ground.

Third-party intervention, on the other hand, encompasses a broader range of activities that extend beyond mediation. It includes diplomatic efforts, arbitration, fact-finding missions, peacekeeping operations, and humanitarian interventions. Third parties can be states, international organizations, non-governmental organizations, or individuals who engage in various roles to facilitate conflict resolution and prevent the escalation of violence.

Mediation and third-party intervention offer numerous benefits in preventing and avoiding war. Firstly, they provide a structured and neutral platform for parties to dialogue, de-escalate tensions, and explore peaceful resolutions. Mediators and third parties help bridge divides and promote reconciliation by facilitating communication and fostering understanding.

Secondly, these approaches enable disputing parties to maintain control over the outcome rather than resort to violent means. Mediation allows parties to actively participate in decision-making and craft solutions that address their underlying interests and concerns. This sense of ownership and empowerment increases the likelihood of sustainable and lasting agreements.

Thirdly, mediation and third-party intervention provide opportunities for the inclusion of diverse perspectives and marginalized voices. By ensuring the representation of all stakeholders, including women, youth, and minority groups, these processes foster inclusivity and promote more comprehensive and representative outcomes.

Key principles guide successful mediation and employ various techniques to facilitate dialogue and resolution. Key principles include impartiality, neutrality, confidentiality, and the voluntary participation of all parties. Mediators create a safe and conducive environment for dialogue, where parties can freely express their concerns and interests.

Techniques used in mediation include active listening, reframing, brainstorming, and exploring creative solutions. Mediators employ these techniques to clarify issues, manage emotions, and facilitate the exploration of mutually beneficial options. By encouraging constructive communication, mediators help parties move beyond entrenched positions and find common ground.

Despite its merits, mediation and third-party intervention face challenges and limitations. One of the primary challenges is the voluntary participation of conflicting parties. In some cases, parties may be reluctant to engage in the process, preferring to pursue their goals through force or other means. Overcoming this challenge requires building trust, ensuring inclusivity, and addressing power imbalances.

Another challenge is the complexity and intractability of some conflicts. Mediators and third parties may encounter deeply rooted grievances, historical animosities, or competing interests that hinder progress. Given the intricacies involved, employing innovative and context-specific approaches that target the root causes of conflict and foster reconciliation is essential.

Additionally, the effectiveness of mediation and third-party intervention is contingent upon the commitment and cooperation of all parties involved. Lack of genuine commitment, insincerity, or a failure to implement agreed-upon solutions can undermine the process and impede the achievement of sustainable peace.

Mediation and third-party intervention play a crucial role in preventing and avoiding war. These strategic approaches provide a platform for dialogue, foster understanding, and empower disputing parties to find peaceful resolutions. By upholding impartiality, confidentiality, and voluntary participation, mediators and third parties can help build trust, bridge divides, and promote reconciliation. However, challenges such as voluntary participation, the complexity of conflicts, and ensuring commitment require careful consideration and adaptive approaches. By harnessing the power of mediation and third-party intervention, we can work towards a world where conflicts are peacefully resolved and the devastating consequences of war are avoided.

THE INVOLVEMENT OF INTERNATIONAL ORGANIZATIONS IN CONFLICT RESOLUTION PLAYS A SIGNIFICANT ROLE

International organizations play a crucial role in addressing conflicts and fostering peace worldwide. With their global reach and impartiality, these organizations provide platforms for dialogue, coordinate peacekeeping efforts, and promote cooperation among nations. International organizations serve as neutral and impartial actors, offering a platform for multilateral dialogue and cooperation.

International organizations, like the United Nations, offer a global platform where member states can come together to tackle conflicts, exchange viewpoints, and pursue peaceful resolutions. Regional organizations, like the African Union (AU) and the European Union (EU), focus on resolving problems in their regions by utilizing their knowledge and closeness to encourage communication and promote reconciliation.

International organizations promote conflict resolution through various mechanisms and tools. One key approach is preventive diplomacy, where organizations engage in early intervention to address emerging conflicts before they escalate into violence. This involves diplomatic efforts, mediation, and the deployment of peacekeeping missions to prevent further hostilities and create conditions for peaceful resolutions.

International organizations' efforts to resolve conflicts sometimes include peacekeeping operations, which are carried out with UN approval. These operations involve the deployment of multinational forces to conflict-affected areas to maintain peace, protect civilians, and facilitate political transitions. In addition to offering protection and fostering an atmosphere favorable to communication and reconciliation, peacekeepers serve as a stabilizing factor.

Furthermore, international organizations contribute to conflict resolution through their expertise and technical assistance. They provide capacity-building support to conflict-affected countries, helping to strengthen governance structures, promote the rule of law, and foster inclusive political processes. They also offer assistance in post-conflict reconstruction and development, addressing the root causes of conflicts and supporting sustainable peacebuilding.

The impact of international organizations in conflict resolution extends beyond immediate peacekeeping efforts. They also promote long-term reconciliation and peacebuilding through transitional justice, human rights, and development initiatives. Transitional justice mechanisms, like truth and reconciliation commissions, are instrumental in establishing accountability, addressing past injustices, and laying the groundwork for healing and reconciliation.

In the preservation of the rights of individuals and communities affected by wars, Amnesty International and Human Rights Watch play a vital role. Their dedication ensures these rights are upheld and protected, advocating for justice and dignity.

Challenges exist in the role of international organizations in conflict resolution. One major challenge is the conflicting' complex, and evolving nature, which requires adaptive and context-specific approaches. Conflicts often involve deep-rooted grievances, ethnic tensions, and political complexities that demand nuanced strategies and sustained engagement.

Another challenge is the limited resources and capacities of international organizations. Peacekeeping operations, for instance, require adequate funding, personnel, and logistical support to carry out their mandates effectively. However, financial constraints, competing priorities, and political divisions among member states can hamper the effectiveness of these operations.

Furthermore, international organizations often face challenges related to political will and the cooperation of conflicting parties. Conflicts may involve actors with divergent interests and agendas, making it difficult to secure all parties' full participation and commitment. Overcoming these challenges requires skillful diplomacy, coordination with regional actors, and sustained engagement to build trust and foster cooperation.

International organizations play a vital role in conflict resolution by providing platforms for dialogue, coordinating peacekeeping efforts, and promoting reconciliation. Their preventive diplomacy, peacekeeping operations, and expertise contribute to preventing and resolving conflicts. International organizations work towards sustainable peacebuilding and a more peaceful world by addressing the root causes of conflicts, upholding human rights, and fostering inclusive processes. Despite challenges, their engagement and coordination with member states, regional bodies, and civil society remain crucial in resolving conflicts and ensuring lasting peace.

PROMOTING UNDERSTANDING AND EMPATHY THROUGH CULTURAL EXCHANGE AND EDUCATION

Promoting understanding and empathy has emerged as a vital strategy for preventing war and fostering peace in a world often marked by conflicts and misunderstandings. Cultural exchange and education are powerful tools to bridge divides, cultivate mutual respect, and build bridges of understanding among diverse communities.

The Power of Cultural Exchange

The power of cultural exchange lies in its ability to transcend borders, bridging gaps between people and fostering deep connections that transcend language and nationality. Through cultural exchange, individuals gain a profound understanding of different customs, traditions, and ways of life. It opens doors to new perspectives, challenges biases, and cultivates a sense of empathy and appreciation for the rich tapestry of human diversity.

When individuals engage in cultural exchange, they step out of their comfort zones and enter a realm of shared experiences. They can immerse themselves in unfamiliar environments, embracing another culture's sights, sounds, tastes, and traditions. By actively participating in the customs and rituals of the host culture, individuals develop a profound appreciation for its uniqueness and begin to see the commonalities that underlie our human experience.

Cultural exchange sparks curiosity and encourages individuals to ask questions, seek knowledge, and engage in meaningful dialogue. It provides a platform for open-minded discussions, where individuals can explore similarities and differences, challenge stereotypes, and build bridges of understanding. By sharing personal stories, struggles, and triumphs, participants in cultural exchange programs create authentic connections that transcend language barriers.

Moreover, cultural exchange fosters a deep respect for cultural heritage and encourages the preservation and promotion of cultural diversity. By experiencing different cultures' arts, music, dance, and literature, individuals gain a newfound appreciation for the richness and beauty of human creativity. This appreciation extends beyond the artistic realm and seeps into everyday interactions, promoting a sense of respect for diverse viewpoints and traditions.

Through cultural exchange, individuals become ambassadors of understanding and advocates for peace. They return to their communities with a broader worldview, equipped with the knowledge and empathy to challenge stereotypes and promote intercultural harmony. By sharing their experiences and encouraging others to embrace cultural exchange, they create a ripple effect of understanding that extends far beyond their immediate surroundings.

The cultural exchange is a powerful catalyst for building bridges and fostering global citizenship. It encourages us to celebrate our differences, find common ground, and work together to create a more inclusive and harmonious world. Cultural exchange empowers us to break down the barriers that separate us and embrace our shared humanity, reminding us that we are all part of a global tapestry woven with threads of diverse cultures, experiences, and aspirations.

The Role of Education

The role of education in promoting understanding and empathy cannot be overstated. It is a powerful tool for shaping individuals' perspectives, challenging biases, and cultivating a sense of empathy and respect for others. Through education, individuals gain a deeper understanding of different cultures, histories, and worldviews, enabling them to navigate an increasingly diverse and interconnected world.

Inclusive and quality education goes beyond imparting knowledge and academic skills. It fosters an environment of respect, acceptance, and appreciation for diversity. By promoting intercultural dialogue and collaboration within educational institutions, students learn to value different perspectives, challenge stereotypes, and develop a sense of empathy toward others.

Education also plays a crucial role in nurturing critical thinking skills for understanding complex social issues and fostering empathy. It encourages students to question assumptions, analyze information from multiple sources, and consider different viewpoints. By equipping individuals with these skills, education empowers them to challenge prejudice and discrimination and to promote inclusivity and social justice.

Furthermore, education teaches the values and principles that underpin peaceful coexistence. It instills a sense of responsibility, respect for human rights, and a commitment to resolving conflicts peacefully.

By learning about historical events, human rights abuses, and the consequences of violence, students develop a deep appreciation for the importance of empathy, compassion, and cooperation in creating a more harmonious and just society.

Education also can break cycles of violence and prejudice by promoting social mobility and empowerment. By providing equal access to education for all, regardless of socioeconomic background, gender, or ethnicity, societies can create opportunities for marginalized individuals to thrive and contribute positively to their communities. Education empowers individuals to overcome stereotypes and discrimination, enabling them to reach their full potential and make meaningful contributions to society.

Intercultural Learning and Global Citizenship

Intercultural learning promotes understanding and empathy by fostering knowledge, skills, and attitudes necessary for respectful and effective interactions with people from diverse backgrounds. It encourages individuals to move beyond their comfort zones, question their assumptions, and embrace new perspectives. Through intercultural learning, individuals can recognize their biases and navigate cultural differences with respect and openness.

Intercultural learning involves more than just acquiring factual knowledge about different cultures. It requires the development of empathy, curiosity, and a willingness to engage in meaningful cross-cultural exchanges. People may widen their perspectives, dispel myths, and develop a profound appreciation for the richness and diversity of human experiences by actively seeking opportunities to learn from others.

Global citizenship is closely intertwined with preventing war. Global citizens understand the interconnectedness of our world and recognize their role in shaping its future. They embrace a sense of responsibility towards all humanity and actively work towards social justice, human rights, and environmental sustainability.

Education that promotes global citizenship equips individuals with the knowledge, skills, and values needed to address global challenges and contribute to positive change. It encourages critical thinking, empathy, and a commitment to social justice. By nurturing a sense of global identity and promoting a deep understanding of the interdependence of nations and peoples, education fosters a sense of shared responsibility and empowers individuals to take action toward a more equitable and peaceful world.

Through intercultural learning and the cultivation of global citizenship, individuals develop the capacity to bridge divides, challenge injustice, and work towards peaceful resolutions of conflicts. They become agents of change, advocating for dialogue, understanding, and cooperation across cultures and borders. By embracing the principles of intercultural learning and global citizenship, we can foster a global community that values diversity, respects human rights, and strives for a future free from the scourge of war.

Challenges and Opportunities

Promoting understanding and empathy through cultural exchange and education presents both challenges and opportunities in building a more inclusive and peaceful world. Language barriers and cultural differences can pose obstacles to effective intercultural dialogue. Unequal access to education, particularly for marginalized communities, limits opportunities for intercultural learning and engagement. Additionally, bias and prejudice deeply rooted in societies can hinder efforts to cultivate empathy and understanding.

To address these challenges, a comprehensive and multifaceted approach is required. First and foremost, investing in inclusive and quality education for all is crucial. Individuals can develop intercultural competencies and embrace diversity by ensuring equal access to education. Education systems should prioritize including diverse perspectives, histories, and cultures, fostering an environment that promotes understanding and empathy.

Cultural exchange initiatives are essential for fostering understanding but must also be reachable, fair, and worthwhile. The removal of obstacles that prohibit people from various backgrounds, particularly those from poor areas, from participating in cultural exchange events is something that must be worked on.

These programs should go beyond surface-level experiences and provide opportunities for authentic and respectful interactions, allowing individuals to engage in genuine dialogue and develop a deeper understanding of different cultures.

Creating safe and inclusive spaces for dialogue is essential in fostering understanding and empathy. Educational institutions should actively promote intercultural understanding, fostering a sense of belonging and respect among students from diverse backgrounds. Initiatives that facilitate cultural exchange, such as community-based events, workshops, and cultural festivals, can also contribute to creating platforms for meaningful interactions.

Technology can be a powerful tool in connecting individuals across borders and promoting intercultural exchange. Virtual platforms can facilitate cross-cultural dialogue, enabling people worldwide to engage in discussions, share experiences, and challenge stereotypes. Leveraging technology effectively can help bridge geographical distances and facilitate connections that promote understanding and empathy.

Collaborative efforts among governments, international organizations, civil society, and educational institutions are crucial in creating an environment for thriving cultural exchange and education. Partnerships can support the development of inclusive policies, sharing best practices, and allocating resources to ensure that cultural exchange and education are prioritized on national and international agendas.

We can create a more inclusive, empathetic, and peaceful world by addressing the challenges and seizing the opportunities presented by cultural exchange and education. Through collective efforts and a commitment to intercultural understanding, we can break down barriers, challenge stereotypes, and build bridges of empathy and compassion across diverse communities.

Impacts and Benefits

The impact of promoting understanding and empathy through cultural exchange and education is far-reaching. These initiatives challenge stereotypes, dismantle prejudice, and promote acceptance by exposing individuals to different cultures, traditions, and perspectives. Individuals develop empathy through personal interactions and shared experiences, fostering a sense of connectedness and common humanity.

Promoting understanding and empathy also contributes to the prevention of war by addressing the root causes of conflict. It reduces ignorance, fear, and mistrust, building bridges of cooperation and collaboration. Cultivating empathy helps individuals see beyond differences and recognize shared aspirations for peace, justice, and prosperity.

Furthermore, the benefits extend beyond individuals to communities and societies. Cultural exchange and education promote social cohesion, inclusivity, and harmony within diverse communities. They foster an appreciation for cultural diversity, contributing to preserving intangible heritage and promoting dialogue between generations. These initiatives create environments conducive to conflict prevention, reconciliation, and sustainable peace by nurturing understanding and empathy.

Promoting understanding and empathy through cultural exchange and education is a powerful means of preventing war and fostering peaceful coexistence. By embracing diversity, challenging biases, and fostering intercultural dialogue, we can bridge divides, nurture empathy, and build a more peaceful world. Investing in inclusive education, supporting cultural exchange programs, and promoting global citizenship are essential steps toward a future where understanding and empathy prevail over conflict and hostility. Let us strive to create a world where a deep appreciation for the richness of human diversity underpins the pursuit of peace.

CHAPTER 3

WEAKNESSES OF THE EXISTING RULES OF WAR

War has been an unfortunate and recurring element of human history, shaping civilizations, redrawing borders, and leaving indelible scars on countless lives. As societies have evolved, so too have the rules that govern the conduct of armed conflicts. Yet, despite the progress made in establishing international frameworks to regulate warfare, the weaknesses inherent in these existing rules have become increasingly evident.

From the ancient codes of conduct etched on clay tablets to the Geneva Conventions that emerged after World War II, the international community has strived to establish norms to limit the brutality and suffering inflicted during conflicts. These rules, known as International Humanitarian Law (IHL), encompass principles such as proportionality, the distinction between combatants and civilians, and the prohibition of certain weapons and tactics. While IHL represents a significant step forward, it remains plagued by various weaknesses that undermine its effectiveness in modern warfare.

The weaknesses inherent in the existing rules of war jeopardize the core objectives of protecting civilians, mitigating suffering, and upholding the principles of justice and accountability. The lack of effective enforcement mechanisms, the struggle to adapt to evolving technologies, and the challenges posed by non-state actors all necessitate a critical examination of IHL and a renewed commitment to its evolution. In the subsequent sections, we will explore these weaknesses in greater detail, shedding light on the urgent need for reform and offering potential avenues for enhancing the efficacy of the rules of war in our complex and ever-changing world.

In this chapter, we will delve into the deficiencies of the current rules of war, uncovering their challenges and the pressing need for comprehensive reform.

LIMITATIONS OF INTERNATIONAL FRAMEWORKS GOVERNING WAR

International frameworks governing war play a crucial role in promoting peace, ensuring human rights, and regulating the conduct of armed conflicts. These frameworks, including international humanitarian law, human rights law, and disarmament treaties, are designed to minimize the suffering caused by war and protect civilians and combatants alike. However, despite their importance, these frameworks have limitations that challenge their effectiveness and implementation. T

Let us look at the limitations of international frameworks governing war, examining their complexities, gaps, and areas for improvement.

- Complexity and Evolving Nature of Armed Conflicts
  Armed conflicts in the modern world have become increasingly complex, presenting a significant limitation to the effectiveness of international war frameworks. These frameworks were primarily designed with the understanding that conflicts would predominantly involve states engaging in traditional forms of warfare. However, the reality is far more intricate, with conflicts now involving various actors, tactics, and motivations.

Non-state actors, such as rebel groups, terrorist organizations, and militias, play a prominent role in many conflicts. Their objectives, strategies, and structures differ greatly from traditional state forces, challenging the assumptions and approaches embedded in existing frameworks. Asymmetric warfare, where one side possesses significantly more power and resources than the other, has also become prevalent. This presents a unique set of challenges in ensuring a fair and balanced approach to conflict resolution and protection of civilian populations.

The blurring of lines between military and civilian spheres further complicates the dynamics of armed conflicts. Combatants may often operate within civilian populations, using them as shields or blending in with non-combatants. This presents a moral and operational dilemma, as international frameworks strive to protect civilians from harm while enabling military operations to target legitimate military objectives. Striking the right balance in such situations requires nuanced and context-specific decision-making, which the existing frameworks may struggle to provide.

Additionally, the evolving nature of technology and warfare challenges international frameworks. The rapid advancement of weaponry, unmanned systems, and cyber capabilities has opened up new frontiers in warfare. These advancements have far-reaching implications, including the potential for increased civilian casualties, privacy infringements, and cyber-attacks. The frameworks must adapt to regulate and mitigate the risks associated with these emerging technologies, ensuring that ethical and legal considerations keep pace with the evolving nature of conflict.

Addressing the limitations of armed conflicts' complexity and evolving nature requires innovative thinking and a willingness to adapt. International organizations, governments, and civil society must engage in ongoing dialogue and collaboration to enhance the existing frameworks and develop new approaches where necessary. This may involve revisiting and updating international treaties, protocols, and guidelines to reflect the realities of modern conflicts better. It also necessitates a deeper understanding of these conflicts' root causes and dynamics, enabling more targeted and effective interventions.

Ultimately, recognizing and addressing the limitations of armed conflicts' complexity and evolving nature is crucial for advancing international frameworks governing war. By doing so, we can ensure that these frameworks remain relevant, effective, and capable of addressing the diverse challenges posed by contemporary conflicts. We can strive for a more peaceful and just world through continuous adaptation and innovation.

- Compliance and Enforcement Challenges
  Compliance and enforcement challenges pose significant limitations to the effectiveness of international frameworks governing war. While these frameworks establish clear rules and regulations, ensuring compliance with them is often complex and multifaceted. Some states may choose to disregard certain provisions or selectively implement them, undermining the overall effectiveness of the frameworks and eroding trust in the international system.

One of the primary challenges is the absence of a strong enforcement mechanism. While international law establishes the legal obligations of states, there is no supranational authority with the power to enforce compliance. This places the burden of enforcement on individual states and the international community. However, enforcing compliance can be politically challenging, particularly in cases where powerful states may have conflicting interests or choose to prioritize their national security concerns.

Another compliance challenge arises from the varying interpretations and understandings of international law among states. The lack of a unified understanding can lead to divergent implementation and inconsistent compliance. States may interpret certain provisions to serve their interests, creating discrepancies in adherence to the frameworks.

Moreover, the complexity and dynamics of armed conflicts present challenges to compliance. In intense conflict, ensuring strict adherence to legal norms and obligations can be difficult. The fog of war, resource constraints, and rapidly changing circumstances may lead to inadvertent violations or deviations from established rules. Additionally, the involvement of non-state actors, who international legal frameworks may not bind, further complicates compliance efforts.

Another major issue is the lack of responsibility for transgressions of international law during wars.

While international courts and tribunals exist to address war crimes and human rights abuses, their jurisdiction and reach may be limited. Political considerations, power imbalances, and challenges in gathering evidence can hinder the prosecution of perpetrators and the delivery of justice to victims.

Addressing compliance and enforcement challenges requires a comprehensive and multifaceted approach. Strengthening the accountability mechanisms and ensuring the availability of robust enforcement mechanisms can act as deterrents and promote compliance. This may involve enhancing the capacity and jurisdiction of international courts, increasing cooperation between states in investigating and prosecuting war crimes, and providing adequate resources and support for these efforts.

Promoting a culture of accountability and respect for international law is also crucial. This can be achieved through awareness-raising campaigns, capacity-building initiatives, and education programs emphasizing the importance of compliance with international norms and the consequences of violations. Strengthening international cooperation and collaboration in monitoring, reporting, and documenting violations can also improve enforcement.

Compliance and enforcement challenges significantly limit the effectiveness of international frameworks governing war. Overcoming these limitations requires a concerted effort by states, international organizations, and civil societies to strengthen enforcement mechanisms, enhance accountability, and promote a culture of compliance with international law. By addressing these challenges, we can create a more just and peaceful world where the rules governing armed conflicts are upheld, and violations are met with appropriate consequences.

- **State Sovereignty and National Security Considerations**
  State sovereignty and national security considerations significantly challenge the effectiveness of international frameworks governing war. The principle of state sovereignty grants states the authority to govern their territories and make decisions for their security. While this principle is essential for maintaining the stability of the international system, it can also limit the willingness of states to comply with international legal obligations in times of conflict fully.

National security concerns often take precedence over international law, as states prioritize the protection of their territory, citizens, and strategic interests. This can lead to reluctance to fully adhere to the provisions of international frameworks, particularly if states believe that compliance may compromise their national security. In such situations, states may employ justifications, such as self-defense or national interest, to circumvent their obligations or interpret international law that aligns with their perceived security imperatives.

The tension between state sovereignty and international legal obligations is especially pronounced in cases where states perceive external interventions or interference as a threat to their sovereignty. The fear of external influence can lead to a defensive stance, causing states to resist international pressure or oversight, even when their actions violate established norms and principles.

Moreover, national security considerations can shape the interpretation and implementation of international law. States may interpret legal provisions favoring their national security interests, potentially leading to divergent understandings and inconsistent compliance. This can undermine the uniform application of international law and create challenges in achieving a cohesive and comprehensive approach to conflict resolution.

Addressing the limitations of state sovereignty and national security considerations requires striking a delicate balance between preserving state sovereignty and promoting international norms and obligations. Recognizing the legitimate security concerns of states is crucial, but it must be done within the framework of international law and with respect for human rights. Efforts should be made to foster a dialogue that reconciles the need for national security with the imperative of upholding international legal principles.

Engaging states in constructive dialogue and highlighting the long-term benefits of compliance with international law can help mitigate the tensions between state sovereignty and international frameworks. Emphasizing the collective security and shared interests of states can encourage a more cooperative approach to conflict resolution. Additionally, providing states with the necessary resources, support, and capacity-building opportunities can assist them in meeting their security needs while adhering to their international legal obligations.

Furthermore, international cooperation and collaboration are essential in addressing the challenges posed by state sovereignty and national security considerations. Encouraging dialogue, building trust, and fostering mutual understanding among states can create an environment conducive to the peaceful resolution of conflicts. Strengthening regional and international mechanisms for conflict prevention and resolution can also provide platforms for addressing the security concerns of states while upholding international legal norms.

State sovereignty and national security considerations challenge the effectiveness of international frameworks governing war. Striking a balance between state sovereignty and international legal obligations is crucial for maintaining stability and promoting compliance with international law. By fostering constructive dialogue, promoting international cooperation, and addressing the legitimate security concerns of states, we can work towards a more harmonious and effective international framework for preventing and resolving conflicts.

- **Limited Scope and Ambiguity in Legal Interpretations**
  Limited scope and ambiguity in legal interpretations of international frameworks governing war present significant challenges to their effective implementation. These challenges arise from the diverse perspectives and interpretations that states and legal scholars bring to understand key concepts and provisions within the frameworks.

One of the main areas of contention is the interpretation of terms such as proportionality and military necessity. Proportionality requires that the harm caused by military action is not excessive in relation to the anticipated military advantage. However, determining what is considered "excessive" or "anticipated military advantage" can vary depending on the context and the parties' interpretation. This ambiguity can create differing interpretations and standards of assessment, leading to inconsistent application of the law and potential violations.

Similarly, the concept of military necessity, which allows for using force in necessary situations to achieve a legitimate military objective, can be subject to varying interpretations. Understanding what constitutes a legitimate military objective can differ, impacting the interpretation of permissible actions during armed conflicts. The ambiguity surrounding these concepts can lead to differing legal opinions and sometimes result in actions that may stretch the boundaries of international legal norms.

Moreover, the limited scope of international legal frameworks governing war can challenge their effectiveness. Traditional frameworks were primarily designed to address state-to-state conflicts, but contemporary conflicts often involve non-state actors, asymmetric warfare, and blurred lines between military and civilian spheres. The existing frameworks struggle to adapt to these changing dynamics, leaving gaps in addressing the unique challenges posed by modern conflicts.

The evolving nature of warfare, such as using new technologies and tactics, further adds to the complexity of legal interpretations. Determining the applicability and interpretation of existing legal frameworks to emerging technologies, such as cyber warfare or autonomous weapons systems, can be challenging. These advancements may require additional legal frameworks or the reinterpretation and adaptation of existing ones to ensure they remain relevant and effective.

To address these limitations, efforts should be made to enhance clarity and consensus in interpreting and applying international legal frameworks. Encouraging dialogue, sharing best practices, and fostering collaboration among states, legal experts, and international organizations can help promote a more consistent and comprehensive understanding of the law. Legal training and capacity-building initiatives can also play a vital role in improving the understanding and implementation of international legal norms.

Furthermore, engaging in ongoing discussions and evaluations is essential to identify gaps and areas for improvement in existing frameworks. Regular reviews and updates can ensure that the law remains responsive to evolving challenges and considers emerging technologies, non-state actors, and the changing nature of armed conflicts. This process requires the active participation and cooperation of states, legal experts, and international organizations to ensure that legal interpretations evolve and adapt to uphold the principles of justice, accountability, and the protection of human rights.

The limited scope and ambiguity in the legal interpretations of international frameworks governing war pose significant challenges to their successful implementation. Addressing these challenges requires enhancing clarity, consensus, and adaptability in interpreting and applying international legal norms. By promoting dialogue, sharing best practices, and undertaking regular reviews, we can work towards a more comprehensive and effective legal framework that upholds the principles of international humanitarian law and contributes to the prevention and resolution of armed conflicts.

- **Technological Advancements and Cyber Warfare**
  Technological advancements have revolutionized how conflicts are waged, with cyber warfare emerging as a significant challenge to the existing international frameworks governing war. The rapid development of technologies, including drones, autonomous weapons systems, and cyber capabilities, has created new capabilities and threats that traditional legal frameworks struggle to address effectively.

Cyber warfare, in particular, presents unique challenges due to its intangible nature and the speed at which attacks can be launched and spread. Unlike traditional warfare, where physical actions and consequences are more easily observable and regulated, cyber-attacks can be conducted remotely, anonymously, and with minimal attribution. This poses challenges in identifying and holding responsible actors accountable for their actions.

The lack of clear guidelines and norms surrounding cyber warfare raises concerns about the potential misuse and unintended consequences of emerging technologies in armed conflicts. Existing international frameworks were primarily designed to address physical aggression between states, and they do not comprehensively cover the complexities of cyber warfare. As a result, there is a need to develop new legal frameworks and norms that specifically address cyber operations, their regulation, and the protection of critical infrastructure and civilians in the cyber domain.

The challenges posed by technological advancements extend beyond cyber warfare. Using drones and autonomous weapons systems raises questions about accountability, proportionality, and the ethical considerations surrounding their deployment. These technologies can potentially change warfare dynamics, but clear regulations must govern their use to prevent unintended harm and minimize civilian casualties.

Addressing these challenges requires international cooperation and dialogue to develop norms and regulations that keep pace with technological advancements. It is crucial to involve states, legal experts, and technology specialists in these discussions to ensure a comprehensive and balanced approach to governing emerging technologies in armed conflicts.

In addition to legal frameworks, there is a need for increased transparency, information sharing, and confidence-building measures among states to reduce the risks associated with technological advancements. Confidence-building measures can help foster trust and cooperation, enhance mutual understanding of capabilities and intentions, and reduce potential misunderstandings or miscalculations that could escalate conflicts.

Moreover, efforts should be made to raise awareness and promote responsible technology use during armed conflicts. Education and training programs can ensure that military personnel, policymakers, and the wider public are well-informed about emerging technologies' implications and ethical considerations.

Technological advancements, including the rise of cyber warfare, present significant challenges not adequately addressed by existing international frameworks governing war. The evolving nature of technology calls for the development of new legal frameworks, norms, and confidence-building measures to ensure the responsible use of emerging technologies and minimize the risks they pose. International cooperation and dialogue are crucial to addressing these challenges and promoting the development of comprehensive and effective regulations that align with the evolving nature of warfare in the digital age.

- **Limited Participation and Representation**
  Limited participation and representation of certain actors in developing and implementing international frameworks governing war can significantly undermine their effectiveness. Traditionally, decision-making processes and negotiations have been monopolized by powerful states, marginalizing the voices of marginalized communities, non-state actors, and civil society organizations. His exclusive strategy falls short of capturing the variety of viewpoints and experiences of individuals who are directly impacted by armed conflicts.

The limited participation of key stakeholders in developing international frameworks can lead to a lack of legitimacy and a skewed representation of interests. It may result in frameworks that do not adequately address the root causes of conflicts, fail to address the needs and concerns of marginalized communities, and neglect the perspectives of those working at the grassroots level to promote peace and reconciliation.

Excluding non-state actors and civil society organizations from the negotiation table overlooks the valuable knowledge and expertise they possess. These actors often deeply understand local dynamics, and their participation can contribute to more comprehensive and context-specific solutions. Their inclusion ensures that the voices of affected communities are heard, their needs are taken into account, and the solutions proposed are sustainable and inclusive.

To overcome this limitation, there is a need for more inclusive and participatory approaches in the development and implementation of international frameworks governing war. This involves creating spaces for dialogue and collaboration that bring together diverse actors, including states, non-state actors, civil society organizations, and local communities. By fostering inclusive processes, decision-making can become more representative, transparent, and accountable.

Inclusivity can be promoted through initiatives prioritizing the participation of marginalized communities, women, youth, and other underrepresented groups. It also requires building bridges between local actors and international institutions, ensuring their knowledge and expertise are integrated into policy discussions and decision-making processes.

International frameworks can benefit from a wider range of perspectives, insights, and solutions by expanding participation and representation. This inclusive approach promotes ownership, legitimacy, and effectiveness in addressing the complex challenges of armed conflicts. It also fosters a sense of empowerment among marginalized communities, strengthening their resilience and agency in pursuing peace and justice.

Limited participation and representation of certain actors in developing and implementing international frameworks governing war present significant limitations to their effectiveness. To overcome this challenge, inclusive and participatory approaches must be embraced, ensuring that the voices of marginalized communities, non-state actors, and civil society organizations are heard and integrated into decision-making processes. By expanding participation and representation, international frameworks can become more comprehensive, responsive, and sustainable in addressing the complexities of armed conflicts.

- **Challenges in Addressing Root Causes and Prevention**
  Challenges arise when international frameworks governing war focus primarily on regulating the conduct of armed conflicts rather than addressing their root causes and preventing their escalation. Conflicts are often deeply rooted in socio-political, economic, and cultural factors that require comprehensive and long-term solutions. The existing frameworks, however, prioritize managing conflicts in the short term, neglecting the underlying causes and thus limiting their effectiveness in preventing future conflicts.

Addressing the root causes of conflicts is crucial for sustainable peace-building and prevention efforts. It involves understanding and tackling inequality, poverty, political instability, ethnic tensions, and resource disputes. These factors are interconnected and require a holistic approach beyond immediate ceasefire agreements and focusing on structural transformation and societal change.

One of the challenges in addressing root causes is the complexity and interplay of various factors. Conflict situations are dynamic and multifaceted, making it difficult to comprehensively identify and address all the underlying causes. It requires a deep understanding of the local context, historical grievances, and power dynamics, which can vary significantly from one conflict to another.

Another challenge is the limited capacity and resources available for preventive efforts. Preventing conflicts requires long-term investments in peace-building, development, and social justice initiatives. However, funding for prevention often takes a back seat to address immediate humanitarian needs or military interventions. This lack of sustained investment hinders the implementation of comprehensive preventive strategies.

Furthermore, the engagement and cooperation of all relevant stakeholders are crucial in addressing root causes and preventing conflicts. This includes governments, civil society organizations, local communities, and international actors. Building trust, fostering dialogue, and promoting inclusive decision-making is key to bringing diverse perspectives together and developing shared solutions.

To overcome these challenges, a shift in mindset and approach is necessary. International frameworks must go beyond crisis management and prioritize conflict prevention as a central component. This involves addressing the root causes of conflicts through investments in education, economic development, good governance, and social inclusion. It also requires a coordinated and integrated approach that brings together diverse actors and resources.

Ultimately, by focusing on prevention and addressing the root causes of conflicts, international frameworks can build more resilient societies and reduce the likelihood of future conflicts. This proactive and comprehensive approach is essential for creating a more peaceful and just world.

- **Inadequate Resources and Capacities**
  The inadequate allocation of resources and capacities poses a significant challenge to effectively implementing international frameworks governing war. Many states, especially those directly affected by conflicts or facing resource constraints, find it difficult to fulfill their obligations and provide the necessary support for compliance with these frameworks.

Financial constraints often hinder states from investing in the infrastructure, training, and personnel needed to implement and enforce international frameworks effectively. Insufficient funds limit the ability to strengthen institutions, conduct necessary research, and establish mechanisms for monitoring and reporting violations. This lack of financial resources can undermine the effectiveness and credibility of the frameworks as states struggle to meet their obligations.

Human resources also play a critical role in implementing and enforcing international frameworks. However, many states face challenges in recruiting and retaining qualified personnel with the necessary expertise in international law, conflict resolution, and human rights areas. The limited availability of skilled professionals can impede the implementation of the frameworks and undermine efforts to address violations and assist affected populations.

Additionally, competing priorities within states can divert attention and resources from implementing international frameworks. States often face numerous pressing issues, such as economic development, public health, and security concerns, which may take precedence over allocating resources for compliance with the frameworks. As a result, the implementation efforts may be fragmented, inconsistent, or insufficiently prioritized.

International cooperation and support are crucial to address the challenge of inadequate resources and capacities. In order to help states achieve their duties, donor nations, international organizations, and civil society may play a crucial role in providing funding, technical assistance, and capacity-building programs. Collaboration and knowledge sharing among states can also help overcome resource limitations by pooling resources, sharing best practices, and promoting collective action.

Moreover, efforts to address the inadequate resources and capacities should focus on long-term sustainability. Building domestic capacities, investing in education and training programs, and strengthening institutional frameworks are essential for ensuring self-reliance and continued compliance with international frameworks. This requires a comprehensive approach that considers each state's specific needs and contexts, as well as the ongoing support and engagement of the international community.

The limitations of international frameworks governing war highlight the challenges in addressing the complexities of armed conflicts, ensuring compliance, and preventing violations of human rights and humanitarian law. While these limitations pose significant obstacles, they also present opportunities for improvement and innovation. Strengthening compliance mechanisms, enhancing accountability, addressing the evolving nature of armed conflicts, promoting meaningful participation, and addressing root causes are crucial steps toward creating more effective and comprehensive frameworks. By continuously evaluating and adapting international frameworks, we can strive for a more just and peaceful world where the suffering caused by war is minimized, and human rights and dignity are protected.

THE ETHICAL DILEMMA OF JUST WAR THEORY

War has been a perennial presence throughout human history, and its ethical considerations have sparked ongoing debates. Just war theory is a framework that seeks to provide ethical guidelines for engaging in armed conflict. However, this theory is not without its ethical dilemmas.

The foundations of just war theory can be traced back to ancient philosophical and religious traditions. Scholars such as Cicero, St. Augustine, and St. Thomas Aquinas contributed to developing this ethical framework, which seeks to reconcile the tension between the desire for peace and the recognition of the need for self-defense and protecting innocent lives. Just war theory consists of several principles that guide the moral evaluation of war. Each of these principles presents its ethical challenges when applied to real-world conflicts.

The principle of just cause states that war is morally justifiable only when there is a legitimate reason for resorting to force. However, determining what constitutes a just cause can be subjective and contentious. Balancing legitimate self-defense, protecting innocent lives, and pursuing national interests can be ethically complex, as competing interpretations of just cause may arise.

According to the concept of proportionality, the anticipated advantages of military action must balance the anticipated costs, including civilian fatalities and devastation. The ethical dilemma lies in accurately assessing and predicting the consequences of war. In the chaos of armed conflict, it is challenging to determine the precise impact of military actions and weigh the potential harms against the desired outcomes.

The principle of discrimination emphasizes distinguishing between combatants and non-combatants, minimizing harm to civilians. Upholding this principle is challenging amid warfare, where the lines between combatants and civilians can become blurred. Balancing military objectives with the duty to protect non-combatants poses ethical dilemmas, particularly when non-state actors and guerrilla tactics are prevalent.

The principle of last resort asserts that war should be a last resort, pursued only when all peaceful means of resolving a conflict have been exhausted. The ethical dilemma lies in determining when all peaceful means have been exhausted and whether diplomatic efforts have been genuinely pursued to their fullest extent. Additionally, the concept of last resort raises questions about the use of preemptive strikes and the ethical implications of preventive war.

The principle of the prohibition on means of warfare prohibits using indiscriminate and excessive force and weapons that cause unnecessary suffering or disproportionately harm civilians. Technological advancements, such as drones and autonomous weapons systems, challenge the application of this principle. The ethical dilemma lies in determining the compatibility of modern warfare with the principles of just war theory and addressing the ethical implications of emerging technologies.

Applying just war theory to real-world conflicts is fraught with challenges. The nature of war itself, with its chaos, uncertainty, and moral ambiguities, poses difficulties in adhering to the principles of just war theory. The fog of war, the pressures of military necessity, and the involvement of non-state actors further complicate ethical decision-making.

Cultural and moral relativism can influence the interpretation and application of just war principles. Different cultures may have varying moral perspectives and understandings of what constitutes a just cause or proportionate response. Bridging these cultural differences and finding common ground in ethical war evaluations can be challenging.

The role of state sovereignty and national security considerations can create tensions between the principles of just war theory and the realities of political decision-making. States often prioritize their national interests and security over strict adherence to ethical principles, leading to ethical dilemmas and questions about the legitimacy of certain military actions.

The ethical dilemmas inherent in just war theory reflect the complexities of applying moral principles to the realities of armed conflict. While just war theory provides a framework for evaluating the morality of war, the challenges of determining just cause, ensuring proportionality, upholding discrimination, and navigating the complexities of modern warfare demand ongoing reflection and debate.

By recognizing these ethical dilemmas, we can engage in meaningful discussions about the ethical implications of armed conflict and work towards developing more comprehensive and nuanced frameworks for evaluating the morality of war. Ultimately, the goal is to minimize the harm and suffering caused by war and strive for a more peaceful and just world.

THE PROLIFERATION OF ASYMMETRIC WARFARE AND NON-STATE ACTORS

Traditional warfare ideas are tested in today's quickly changing global environment by the development of asymmetric warfare and the rise of non-state actors.

Asymmetric warfare refers to conflicts in which the belligerents have significantly different military capabilities and strategies while non-state actors operate independently of recognized state authorities.

A significant power imbalance between the opposing forces characterizes asymmetric warfare. While one side may possess conventional military capabilities, the other often employs unconventional tactics, strategies, and weaponry. This asymmetry can take various forms, including guerrilla warfare, insurgencies, terrorism, and cyber warfare. Non-state actors, such as rebel groups, terrorist organizations, and criminal networks, often engage in asymmetric warfare as they lack state actors' resources and conventional military strength.

Several factors have facilitated the rise of non-state actors. Globalization has interconnected societies and facilitated the flow of ideas, resources, and technology across borders, enabling non-state actors to operate on a transnational scale. Technological advancements, particularly in communication and transportation, have enhanced the ability of these actors to coordinate and execute their operations. Additionally, the breakdown of traditional state structures in some regions has created power vacuums that non-state actors exploit to gain influence and control.

One significant aspect of non-state actors is their ability to exploit power asymmetry and employ unconventional tactics. Their agility, adaptability, and ability to blend into local populations make them difficult to identify and counter. Moreover, non-state actors can leverage modern communication technologies to spread their message, recruit supporters, and coordinate attacks, posing unique challenges to state actors.

The proliferation of asymmetric warfare and the rise of non-state actors have significant implications for global security. Traditional state-centric approaches to warfare, which emphasize conventional military forces, may be ill-suited to counter the threats posed by non-state actors. These actors often operate in complex environments characterized by civilian populations, urban settings, and decentralized networks, making it challenging for conventional militaries to target them effectively without causing significant collateral damage.

Furthermore, the motivations and objectives of non-state actors differ from those of traditional state actors. While states may engage in warfare to protect their national interests or pursue political goals, non-state actors often have ideological, religious, or extremist agendas. This ideological dimension adds another layer of complexity to the conflict, making it difficult to address through conventional military means alone.

Addressing the challenges of asymmetric warfare and non-state actors requires a multifaceted approach. Intelligence and information-sharing among states are crucial for understanding non-state actors' networks, capabilities, and intentions. Collaboration and coordination between military forces, intelligence agencies, law enforcement agencies, and international organizations are necessary to effectively disrupt the activities of non-state actors and prevent their proliferation.

Counterinsurgency strategies that focus on winning the hearts and minds of local populations can also play a significant role in countering non-state actors. By addressing the underlying grievances and socio-economic factors that contribute to the rise of these actors, states can undermine their support base and diminish their appeal to marginalized communities.

Moreover, efforts to combat asymmetric warfare and non-state actors must also address the root causes that give rise to these conflicts. Socio-political instability, economic disparities, and social exclusion can create fertile ground for the emergence of non-state actors. Investing in long-term development, good governance, and conflict resolution mechanisms can help address these root causes and reduce the likelihood of violent conflicts.

The proliferation of asymmetric warfare and the rise of non-state actors present significant challenges to global security. Their ability to exploit power imbalances, employ unconventional tactics and operate independently of recognized state authorities requires a reevaluation of traditional approaches to warfare. Addressing these challenges necessitates international cooperation, intelligence-sharing, counterinsurgency strategies, and efforts to address the root causes of conflicts. By understanding and adapting to the changing nature of warfare, states can better navigate the complexities posed by asymmetric warfare and non-state actors, ultimately contributing to a more stable and secure world.

THE IMPACT OF TECHNOLOGICAL ADVANCEMENTS ON WARFARE AND CIVILIAN CASUALTIES

Throughout history, technological developments have had a significant influence on warfare. New technologies have influenced how wars are waged, from the creation of nuclear weapons to the discovery of gunpowder.

Rapid advancements in various fields, such as information technology, robotics, and precision weaponry, have revolutionized warfare in recent decades. While these advancements offer potential benefits regarding military effectiveness and operational capabilities, they raise ethical concerns, particularly regarding civilian casualties.

The Evolution of Warfare

Throughout history, warfare has been shaped by advancements in technology. From primitive tools like swords and spears to the development of firearms, each new technological innovation has significantly impacted how wars are fought. These advancements have altered the dynamics of conflict, from the tactics and strategies employed on the battlefield to the overall conduct and scale of warfare.

In ancient times, battles were fought primarily through close-quarters combat using handheld weapons. The introduction of bronze and iron weapons revolutionized warfare, enabling armies to inflict greater damage and engage in more prolonged conflicts. The development of siege engines, such as battering rams and catapults, allowed for the assault and defense of fortified positions, leading to the rise of walled cities and fortifications as key strategic assets.

The Middle Ages saw the invention of gunpowder, a major turning point in warfare development.

Battle tactics were changed with the introduction of firearms, such as cannons and muskets. They provided armies with increased firepower and range, leading to changes in tactics, formations, and defensive strategies. This era saw the decline of heavily armored knights and the rise of professional standing armies.

The 18th and 19th centuries Industrial Revolution saw a fresh wave of technical developments that significantly altered warfare.

The invention of steam power and railways revolutionized logistics and transportation, enabling armies to mobilize and deploy more rapidly. The development of rifled muskets, artillery, and warships, coupled with the widespread use of mass production techniques, led to larger and more destructive conflicts, such as the American Civil War and World War I.

The 20th century witnessed unprecedented advancements in warfare technology, particularly during the two World Wars. The introduction of tanks, aircraft, chemical weapons, and submarines reshaped the battlefield and brought new dimensions to warfare. These technological innovations allowed for rapid maneuverability, long-range bombardment, and the ability to inflict mass destruction on a scale never seen before.

Technological change has accelerated even further in recent decades with the rise of information technology and the digital age. The development of computers, satellites, communication networks, and unscrewed aerial vehicles (UAVs) has ushered in a new era of warfare. Information technology has enabled real-time communication, surveillance, and intelligence gathering, providing military forces with enhanced situational awareness and decision-making capabilities.

The increased use of drones and unmanned systems has also transformed how wars are conducted. These technologies allow for remote operations, reducing the risk to military personnel and enabling precision strikes on targets. However, they also raise ethical concerns, particularly regarding civilian casualties and the potential for indiscriminate use.

Emerging technologies like robots, artificial intelligence, cyber warfare, and autonomous weapon systems will probably have a big impact on how war is fought in the future. Emerging technologies like robots, artificial intelligence, cyber warfare, and autonomous weapon systems will probably have a big impact on how war is fought in the future.

These advancements present new opportunities for military effectiveness but also pose complex ethical dilemmas. Questions about the appropriate use of emerging technologies, the role of human judgment in decision-making, and the accountability for actions in warfare continue to challenge policymakers, military strategists, and ethicists.

Information Technology and Cyber Warfare

One of the most significant advancements in recent times is the rise of information technology and its impact on warfare. The interconnectedness of modern societies and reliance on digital infrastructure have made cyber warfare a potent tool. State and non-state actors can launch cyber-attacks to disrupt critical systems, infiltrate databases, and wage covert operations. The consequences of cyber warfare extend beyond traditional battlefields, potentially impacting civilian infrastructure and disrupting essential services.

Precision Guided Munitions

Precision-guided munitions, such as guided missiles and smart bombs, have revolutionized warfare by allowing precise targeting of military objectives. These weapons are designed to minimize collateral damage and civilian casualties by accurately hitting intended targets. However, challenges remain in ensuring the accuracy of targeting information and verifying the presence of civilians in the vicinity of the target. Mistakes or deliberate misuse of these weapons can still result in unintended harm to civilians and infrastructure.

Challenges in Mitigating Civilian Casualties

Despite the potential benefits of technological advancements, the ethical challenges in minimizing civilian casualties persist. Several factors contribute to these challenges:

1. **Lack of Precision and Intelligence:** While precision-guided weapons have improved accuracy, challenges remain in gathering accurate intelligence about the presence of civilians in conflict zones. The fog of war, misinformation, and deliberate concealment by adversaries make it difficult to ensure the safety of non-combatants.

2. **Blurred Lines of Conflict:** Modern warfare often involves asymmetric conflicts where non-state actors operate within civilian populations. Distinguishing combatants from non-combatants becomes challenging as non-state actors blend in with local communities, using them as shields or leveraging their support. This blurring of lines increases the risk of civilian casualties.

3. **Rapid Technological Advancements:** The rapid pace of technological advancements outpaces the development of legal and ethical frameworks to govern their use. This creates a gap in accountability and raises concerns about the appropriate use of emerging technologies in warfare.

4. **Psychological Impacts and Post-Traumatic Stress:** Technological advancements have introduced new psychological challenges for soldiers. Remote warfare, where operators engage in combat from a distance, can lead to detachment and dehumanization, potentially increasing the risk of indiscriminate actions and civilian harm.

Mitigating Civilian Casualties

Mitigating civilian casualties in modern warfare requires a comprehensive and multifaceted approach. Some key considerations include:

1. **Adherence to International Humanitarian Law:** States must abide by international humanitarian law, including the principles of distinction, proportionality, and precautions in attack. These principles ensure that military actions are directed at legitimate targets, the use of force is proportionate to the military objective, and all feasible precautions are taken to minimize harm to civilians.

2. **Enhanced Intelligence and Surveillance:** Improvements in intelligence gathering and surveillance technologies can help identify combatants and distinguish them from non-combatants. Advanced sensors, satellite imagery, and real-time information sharing can assist in minimizing civilian harm.

3. **Ethical Use of Autonomous Weapons:** The development and use of autonomous weapons systems must adhere to strict ethical guidelines. Ensuring human oversight, accountability, and clear

rules of engagement are essential to prevent unintended harm to civilians.

4. **Humanitarian Aid and Reconstruction:** Supporting post-conflict humanitarian efforts and reconstruction initiatives can help mitigate the impact of warfare on civilian populations. Providing essential services, medical assistance, and psychological support can aid in rebuilding communities and facilitating long-term recovery.

Technological advancements have transformed the nature of warfare, offering new capabilities and challenges. While these advancements can potentially enhance military effectiveness, they raise ethical concerns regarding civilian casualties. Striking a balance between military objectives and the protection of non-combatants requires a comprehensive approach that includes adherence to international humanitarian law, enhanced intelligence capabilities, ethical use of autonomous weapons, and post-conflict support. Addressing these challenges and promoting responsible use of technology in warfare can mitigate the impact on civilian populations and foster a more ethical approach to modern conflict.

CHAPTER 4

PEACE ACCORDS AND ADVANTAGES

A peace accord, also known as a peace agreement, is a formal agreement between two or more parties involved in a conflict or dispute to end hostilities and establish a lasting peace. These agreements are crucial in resolving conflicts and preventing further violence and instability.

Peace accords can be negotiated to end various conflicts, including armed conflicts, civil wars, territorial disputes, and political or ideological confrontations. They can be signed between governments and rebel groups, between countries, or even within a single country among different factions.

Reaching a peace accord typically involves negotiations, mediation, and diplomacy. Neutral third-party mediators, international organizations, or diplomats may assist in facilitating the talks and finding common ground between the conflicting parties.

Peace is the delicate melody that humanity yearns for, a symphony of harmony and tranquility that resonates within the hearts of people across the globe. The absence of violence, conflict, and the horrors of war allows societies to flourish and individuals to thrive. In essence, peace represents humanity's collective aspiration to live in a world where differences are celebrated, and conflicts are resolved through dialogue rather than bloodshed.

Yet, achieving peace is no simple task. It requires a concerted effort from all corners of the world, as the pursuit of peace knows no boundaries. Whether on a global scale, encompassing nations and governments, or on a local level involving communities and individuals, the ultimate goal remains: creating an environment where peace becomes the cornerstone of existence.

In this noble endeavor, the Peace Accord emerges as a powerful instrument, offering a glimmer of hope amidst the chaos and discord that plagues our world. It is a formal agreement, a sacred pact between conflicting parties, bound by the shared desire to resolve conflicts, prevent the eruption of war, and nurture the seeds of stability.

The significance of Peace Accords lies in their ability to transcend the barriers erected by hatred, fear, and misunderstanding. They represent a bridge built upon diplomacy, negotiation, and compromise, connecting divergent perspectives and interests. These agreements embody the belief that dialogue, rather than violence, can lead to a resolution satisfying all parties' aspirations.

On a global level, Peace Accords serve as the linchpin preventing catastrophic wars between nations. They stand as testaments to the power of diplomacy, which can extinguish the fires of conflict and pave the way for peaceful coexistence. Through treaties such as the Treaty of Westphalia, which brought an end to the devastating Thirty Years' War, or the Geneva Conventions, which established principles for the humane treatment of individuals in times of armed conflict, Peace Accords have proven their worth time and again in preserving global peace.

At the local level, Peace Accords play an equally vital role in quelling the flames of internal conflicts that threaten the very fabric of societies. They provide an avenue for dialogue and reconciliation, enabling divided communities to heal the wounds of the past and embrace a future built upon shared understanding and cooperation. Examples like the Good Friday Agreement, which ended the sectarian violence in Northern Ireland, or the Comprehensive Peace Agreement in Nepal, which laid the foundation for lasting peace after a decade-long civil war, demonstrate the transformative power of local Peace Accords.

The Peace Accord is a beacon of hope, a tangible embodiment of our collective yearning for peace. It symbolizes the capacity of humanity to rise above differences and seek common ground. It is a testament to our belief that conflicts can be resolved without violence and that stability and progress can emerge from the ashes of discord.

However, Peace Accords alone are not a panacea. They require commitment, perseverance, and the genuine willingness of all parties involved to honor the terms of the agreement. The road to peace is often arduous and filled with obstacles, but it is through unwavering dedication to dialogue, understanding, and justice that we can forge a world where peace reigns supreme.

THE ABRAHAM ACCORDS AND SUCCESSFUL REGIONAL PEACE AGREEMENTS

In the annals of history, pursuing peace has been a constant struggle in regions plagued by strife and political complexities. However, glimmers of hope emerge with successful regional peace agreements, showcasing the art of diplomacy, pragmatism, and shared interests. A prominent example is the Abraham Accords, signed in 2020, which brought Israel, the United Arab Emirates (UAE), and Bahrain together in a meaningful agreement facilitated by the United States.

The genesis of the Abraham Accords can be attributed to shifting dynamics in the Middle East, where the common enemy of Iran united these nations in pursuit of regional stability. Moreover, economic opportunities were a driving force, envisioning shared prosperity through cooperation in various sectors.

The success of the Abraham Accords lies in direct negotiations, a pragmatic approach, and an incremental process. The parties built mutual trust and confidence over time by focusing on practical issues and shared interests.

Looking beyond the Middle East, other successful regional peace agreements offer valuable insights. The Camp David Accords in 1978 showcased the importance of bold leadership and significant concessions. The Good Friday Agreement in 1998 emphasized inclusivity and addressing the root causes of conflict through political reforms.

However, challenges persist, such as needing a long-term commitment, navigating public opinion, and managing external interference. Security concerns must also be addressed to maintain trust and sustainability.

In Northern Ireland, the Good Friday Agreement ended decades of conflict and demonstrated the significance of inclusivity and power-sharing. By involving various stakeholders and addressing the root causes of the conflict through political reforms, the agreement paved the way for a more stable and peaceful Northern Ireland.

Another important step toward achieving peace is the Oslo Accords, which were reached by Israel and the Palestine Liberation Organization (PLO). The covert talks and temporary agreements served as a reminder of the value of discrete diplomacy and the gradual settlement of problems in complicated situations.

Similarly, the Peace Agreement in Mozambique, signed in 1992, ended the country's civil war. Key to its success was the implementation of disarmament, demobilization, and reintegration (DDR) programs, which allowed former combatants to reintegrate into society peacefully.

While the examples of successful peace agreements are encouraging, the challenges faced during the implementation phase cannot be overlooked. Sustainable peace requires unwavering commitment from all parties involved. Without long-term dedication, agreements can unravel, leading to renewed hostilities.

Moreover, public opinion plays a significant role in shaping the success of peace agreements. Leaders must navigate domestic sentiments and effectively communicate the benefits of peace to their populations. Public support is crucial for sustaining peace efforts and overcoming obstacles that may arise during implementation.

External interference can also complicate peace processes. The involvement of countries with vested interests in the region can introduce complexities and undermine the delicate balance of negotiations. Striking a balance that ensures regional ownership of the peace process while incorporating international support is vital for long-term success. Additionally, addressing security concerns is crucial to maintaining trust between parties. Providing safety guarantees during the implementation phase is paramount, as any security breaches can lead to a breakdown in trust and derail the peace process.

Successful regional peace agreements like the Abraham Accords, the Camp David Accords, the Good Friday Agreement, the Oslo Accords, and the Mozambique Peace Agreement demonstrate the possibility of achieving peace through dialogue, cooperation, and pragmatic approaches. These agreements provide valuable lessons that can guide future peace efforts in conflict-affected regions worldwide.

As the world continues to grapple with longstanding conflicts, the significance of these agreements cannot be overstated. The pursuit of peace requires collective efforts, determined leadership, and international support. By learning from successful examples and addressing challenges proactively, humanity can move closer to realizing a more peaceful and harmonious world for future generations.

ECONOMIC COOPERATION AND TRADE BENEFITS

In a world rife with conflicts and geopolitical tensions, pursuing peace has always been a paramount goal for nations and international organizations. Peace accords, as formal agreements to end hostilities and promote amicable relations hold the potential to unlock economic opportunities and trade benefits among the involved parties. Beyond the immediate cessation of violence, peace accords pave the way for economic cooperation, investment, and regional integration, transforming conflict-ridden regions into thriving centers of economic prosperity.

The Genesis of Economic Cooperation

Peace accords are critical milestones in the often tumultuous relations between conflicting parties. When these agreements are reached, they mark a turning point where former adversaries have a unique opportunity to shift gears and engage in economic collaborations and trade relations that were previously unfeasible due to deep-rooted tensions and hostilities. Resolving disputes and establishing diplomatic relations in the aftermath of peace accords set the stage for enhanced economic cooperation, creating a fertile ground for prosperity and development.

One of the fundamental pillars of economic cooperation resulting from peace accords lies in dismantling trade barriers, tariffs, and quotas. As nations embrace peace, they recognize the potential for economic growth and activity by opening up markets and facilitating the movement of goods and services. Countries encourage cross-border trade, investment, and the free flow of commerce by eliminating or reducing trade barriers. This increased market access fosters the growth of businesses, promotes innovation, and encourages entrepreneurship.

Furthermore, lifting trade barriers and tariffs bolsters consumer welfare, allowing access to a broader range of products at competitive prices. Consumers benefit from a more diverse array of goods and services, leading to an improved quality of life. Additionally, removing barriers can lower production costs for industries, making their products more affordable and accessible on the global market.

Economic cooperation facilitated by peace accords also opens up opportunities for cross-border investments. As peace prevails, governments and businesses gain the confidence to plan for the long term. Domestic and international investors are more inclined to commit capital in regions that offer a stable and secure environment. Predictability becomes a key driver for investment decisions, with long-term prospects becoming more favorable without geopolitical uncertainties.

Investment, in turn, catalyzes economic development and contributes to job creation. In post-conflict regions, where rebuilding is essential, foreign direct investment (FDI) can be crucial in revitalizing economies and providing much-needed employment opportunities. Moreover, peace accords often encourage investments in sectors that were previously inaccessible or perceived as risky, leading to the diversification and expansion of industries.

Another significant aspect of economic cooperation resulting from peace accords is fostering regional integration. Peaceful coexistence encourages collaboration and coordination among neighboring countries. Economic integration can lead to the formation of regional blocs, promoting cross-border infrastructure projects, and establishing common regulatory frameworks. Creating regional economic communities enhances the region's attractiveness for trade and investment, creating a win-win situation for all involved parties.

Peace accords often include provisions for economic development and reconstruction efforts in conflict-affected areas. Infrastructure development projects, such as roads, ports, and energy facilities, not only contribute to the region's economic growth but also promote regional connectivity and trade. By investing in infrastructure, countries can leverage their geographic location and transform themselves into logistical hubs, attracting businesses and investors seeking access to multiple markets.

Furthermore, economic cooperation resulting from peace accords can transcend borders and lead to collaborations in technology, research, and innovation. As nations put their differences aside and focus on mutual interests, they can leverage each other's strengths to drive advancements in science, technology, and various industries. Such collaborations can result in groundbreaking discoveries, technological advancements, and sharing best practices across borders.

Case Studies of Successful Economic Cooperation Resulting from Peace Accords:

- The European Union (EU) - A Model of Economic Integration
  The European Union is one of the most remarkable examples of economic cooperation and trade benefits from peace accords. After the devastation of World War II, visionary leaders sought to prevent future conflicts and promote economic cooperation.

Establishing the EU's single market allowed member states to enjoy the unrestricted movement of goods, services, capital, and labor. This integration has facilitated seamless trade, investment, and cross-border business collaborations, leading to economic growth and shared prosperity.

The EU's regional integration model serves as a template for other regions seeking to enhance economic cooperation through peace accords. By building a sense of interdependence among European nations, the EU has effectively reduced the likelihood of conflicts between member states.

- The Colombia Peace Agreement - Unleashing Economic Potential
  In 2016, a transformative peace accord unfolded, bridging the Colombian government and the Revolutionary Armed Forces of Colombia (FARC) and surprisingly unraveling the seeds of economic potential amidst the aftermath of conflict.

Following the signing of the peace accord, steps were taken to encourage rural development, addressing the fundamental causes of the war. Investment in agriculture, infrastructure, and social programs has revitalized rural areas, unlocking their economic potential and empowering local communities.

Improved security in formerly conflict-affected regions has led to a surge in tourism, attracting both domestic and international visitors. Additionally, increased investor confidence has resulted in substantial foreign direct investment (FDI) across various sectors, further contributing to economic growth and job creation.

The peace agreement has also led to enhanced trade within the region. Reducing barriers and tensions has opened up new export opportunities for Colombian goods and services, bolstering the country's international trade prospects.

- The Abraham Accords - Fostering Economic Synergy in the Middle East
  An era of economic cooperation and trade advantages in the Middle East began due to the Abraham Accords, signed in 2020 by Israel, Bahrain, and the United Arab Emirates (UAE).

The agreement has facilitated the exchange of technology and innovation between Israel and the Gulf states. Joint ventures and partnerships have emerged, leveraging each other's expertise to drive economic growth and technological advancements.

Energy cooperation has become a focal point of the accords, with opportunities for resource-sharing and mutual energy security strategies. The alignment of interests in the energy sector has further strengthened economic ties between the involved nations.

The normalization of relations has attracted significant foreign investment to the region. Gulf investors are increasingly exploring opportunities in Israel's dynamic start-up ecosystem, while Israeli companies benefit from access to Gulf markets and capital.

Economic cooperation and trade benefits resulting from peace accords are pivotal in transforming conflict-ridden regions into flourishing hubs of economic prosperity. As exemplified by the EU's post-WWII success, the Colombia Peace Agreement, and the Abraham Accords, peace accords avert hostilities and create an environment conducive to economic growth, investment, and regional integration.

Through trade opportunities, enhanced investment climate, infrastructure development, job creation, and overall economic growth, peace accords unlock the economic potential of nations and foster lasting peace. As we look to the future, international actors, governments, and policymakers need to continue investing in peace-building efforts and nurturing economic cooperation, recognizing that economic interdependence can be a powerful tool in preventing conflicts and advancing global prosperity.

By prioritizing peaceful resolution and investing in economic cooperation, humanity can move closer to a world where prosperity, stability, and peace prevail. Through collaboration and collective efforts, nations can harness the dividends of peace and create a more interconnected and prosperous global community.

ENHANCED SECURITY AND STABILITY IN CONFLICT REGIONS

In the tumultuous landscapes of conflict regions, where violence and discord have prevailed, a glimmer of hope emerges when nations and factions decide to lay down their arms and seek peace by signing peace accords. These agreements represent more than just a cessation of hostilities; they hold the transformative potential to enhance security and stability in regions torn apart by strife and animosity.

Peace accords are symbols of hope, resulting from parties' willingness to set aside their differences and seek a resolution peacefully. These agreements, which signify a dedication to breaking the cycle of violence and creating a road to security and stability, result from the fortitude to engage in discourse and establish common ground.

Addressing Root Causes of Conflict

Addressing conflicts' root causes lies at the essence of peace accords. These agreements provide a safe and constructive platform for conflicting parties to confront historical grievances, social injustices, and unmet political aspirations fueling violence and hostility. Through open dialogue and genuine understanding, the seeds of reconciliation and sustainable peace can finally take root.

The process of delving into the past is courageous, as it requires parties to face painful truths and confront the legacy of conflict. However, this process paves a transformative journey toward healing and reconciliation. By acknowledging the complexities of their shared history, conflicting parties gain a deeper understanding of each other's perspectives, fostering empathy and compassion.

In this crucible of dialogue, peace accords go beyond superficial Band-Aid solutions. They lay the groundwork for lasting peace by addressing the root causes perpetuating the cycle of violence. The hostile boundaries blur as participants come to terms with their history, making room for cooperation and collaboration.

Through this profound endeavor, peace accords shape a new narrative for the future. They plant the seeds of hope and trust, nurturing the vision of a society free from the shackles of historical animosities. By acknowledging and addressing the root causes, peace accords lay the foundation for a more equitable and harmonious future, where the scars of conflict can gradually heal, and the potential for sustainable peace can be fully realized.

Disarmament, Demobilization, and Reintegration (DDR) Programs
Disarmament, demobilization, and reintegration (DDR) programs play a pivotal role in building security and stability in conflict regions. Through these initiatives, former combatants are disarmed, transforming from warriors to contributors to society. Reintegration into civilian life through education, skills training, and employment opportunities reduces the risk of renewed violence but also aids in rebuilding shattered communities.

Transitional Justice Mechanisms
Peace accords often incorporate provisions for transitional justice mechanisms, such as truth commissions and special courts. These

mechanisms offer a path to accountability for human rights abuses and atrocities committed during conflicts. Acknowledging the past and seeking justice for victims fosters a sense of closure, laying the groundwork for a more just and stable society.

Confidence-Building Measures

Confidence-building measures stand as essential pillars in the edifice of peace accords. In the aftermath of conflict, when trust is fragile, and wounds are raw, these measures serve as bridges towards reconciliation and cooperation. Ceasefires signal a cessation of hostilities, a momentary respite in which adversaries can envision a different future. On the other hand, prisoner exchanges embody a tangible act of goodwill, reflecting a commitment to understanding the pain and suffering experienced by both sides.

Moreover, establishing neutral zones represents the willingness to lay down arms and engage in dialogue. In this safe space, parties can start to see each other not solely as adversaries but as human beings with shared aspirations for peace and prosperity.

By undertaking these confidence-building measures, conflicting parties sow the seeds of mutual respect and understanding. Confidence slowly takes root, allowing the delicate shoots of cooperation and dialogue to flourish. In this atmosphere of newfound trust, the groundwork for a durable and inclusive peace is laid, opening the path toward a future where conflicts are resolved through dialogue rather than violence.

Involvement of Regional and International Actors

The participation of regional and international players greatly aids Peace agreements' legitimacy and success.

As impartial mediators, regional organizations and international bodies ensure that all parties are represented and heard during negotiations.

Their presence is a deterrent against potential spoilers seeking to disrupt peace. Additionally, these actors provide essential resources, expertise, and logistical support, which are crucial in implementing the peace agreement effectively. Their commitment strengthens the credibility of the accords and enhances the prospects of a sustainable and inclusive peace, bolstering the chances of a brighter future for conflict-affected regions.

Cross-Border Cooperation and Regional Security

Following the signing of peace accords, neighboring countries are often compelled to embrace cross-border cooperation and regional security initiatives. In a post-conflict landscape, the imperative of regional solidarity becomes evident as nations recognize the shared vulnerabilities and opportunities for collective growth.

Working together to confront transnational dangers likes terrorism and arms trafficking acts as a uniting factor that cuts beyond national boundaries. Previously permeable borders have transformed into strengthened barricades against shared foes, fostering a feeling of cooperation and mutual confidence. These security alliances improve the efficiency of counterterrorism measures and promote unity among once hostile states.

Regional security cooperation is a powerful deterrent against spoilers seeking to disrupt the peace. The collective vigilance of neighboring nations serves as a bulwark against a potential resurgence of conflict. In this atmosphere of trust and shared interests, the chances of disputes escalating into violence are significantly reduced.

Moreover, cross-border cooperation extends beyond security concerns and economic development and infrastructural projects. Collaborative efforts in these areas lay the foundation for regional prosperity and integration, enhancing stability further.

As nations pool their resources and expertise, regional security cooperation becomes a formidable force for safeguarding peace. The collective resolve to uphold stability ensures that peace does not remain confined within national boundaries but extends its protective embrace across the entire region.

In adversity, peace accords provide hope for a brighter future. They exemplify the power of diplomacy and dialogue to pave the way for security, stability, and reconciliation. As we strive for global peace, let us remember that the journey toward security and stability begins with the collective commitment to seek peaceful resolutions and embrace the transformative potential of peace accords.

STRENGTHENING DIPLOMATIC TIES AND FOSTERING CULTURAL UNDERSTANDING

Peace accords are not merely instruments to end conflicts; they can transform the dynamics between nations and foster a deeper sense of mutual understanding and cultural appreciation. The journey toward peace requires diplomacy, compromise, and empathy, and it is through this process that diplomatic ties are strengthened and cultural barriers are dismantled.

At the heart of peace accords lies the commitment to dialogue and negotiation. As conflicting parties engage in discussions to resolve, they learn to listen to each other's perspectives and concerns. This exchange of ideas creates a space for open communication and the building of diplomatic ties. When nations can sit together at the negotiating table, they are willing to find common ground and work towards a shared future.

As peace accords are reached, the newfound diplomatic ties extend beyond the confines of the agreement itself. Coming together to seek peace creates a foundation for future cooperation and engagement.

Once strained by conflict, diplomatic channels are now lubricated with a sense of trust and shared objectives.

Moreover, peace accords often involve the establishment of diplomatic missions and embassies in each other's territories. These diplomatic outposts serve as physical manifestations of the commitment to peaceful relations and pave the way for a deeper exchange of ideas, culture, and knowledge. Ambassadors become bridges between nations, nurturing diplomatic ties on a personal level.

Cultural understanding is a vital byproduct of the peace process. As nations seek to resolve conflicts, they face each other's cultures, histories, and traditions. In this journey, stereotypes are shattered, and misconceptions are dispelled. The recognition of cultural diversity becomes a source of strength rather than division.

In the aftermath of peace accords, cultural exchange programs often flourish. Nations gain insight into each other's heritage and values through educational exchanges, art exhibitions, and cultural festivals. This cultural appreciation fosters a deep respect for diversity and creates a shared space for dialogue and collaboration.

Peace accords also provide opportunities for reconciliation and healing at the grassroots level. People-to-people interactions become catalysts for understanding and empathy. Individuals from conflicting nations come together to share their stories and experiences, walls of misunderstanding are broken down, and bridges of understanding are built.

Cultural diplomacy becomes an invaluable tool in maintaining lasting peace. Nations can leverage the power of culture to build bridges and promote dialogue. From cultural exchange programs to joint artistic ventures, culture is a universal language that transcends borders and unites people in their shared humanity.

Peace accords are not merely legal documents but transformative agents that strengthen diplomatic ties and foster cultural understanding. Through the commitment to dialogue and compromise, nations build trust and respect, laying the groundwork for lasting peace. As diplomatic channels are revitalized, nations find new avenues for collaboration and cooperation. Cultural understanding becomes a natural outgrowth of the peace process as people from conflicting nations come together, share their stories, and break down barriers of prejudice. Ultimately, through the power of peace accords, nations learn to see each other not as adversaries but as partners in a shared journey toward a future of harmony and understanding.

CHAPTER 5

ANALYZING FAILED PEACE ACCORDS

Pursuing peace has always been a paramount objective for nations worldwide in international relations. Historically, conflicts have arisen due to competing interests, territorial disputes, and ideological differences, often devastating consequences for combatants and civilians. In an effort to curtail the outbreak and escalation of hostilities, peace accords have been crafted and implemented, aiming to bring about peaceful resolutions and sustainable solutions. However, amidst the noble intent behind these accords, failures have been encountered, leaving societies to grapple with the persistent specter of conflict.

This analysis delves into the intricacies of failed peace accords, aiming to discern the underlying reasons that undermine their efficacy. By examining the weaknesses of the existing rules of war, it becomes evident that nations must reconsider their approaches to conflict resolution and prioritize the pursuit of peace. In doing so, they mitigate human suffering and foster an environment conducive to prosperity, development, and cooperation on the global stage. Through comprehensive examination and discussion, this chapter sheds light on the imperatives for nations to opt for peace and forge durable agreements that stand the test of time.

FACTORS CONTRIBUTING TO THE FAILURE OF PEACE AGREEMENTS

In the annals of human civilization, conflicts and wars have regrettably been a ubiquitous presence, inflicting immense suffering and widespread destruction upon nations and societies. In response to these adversities, the quest for peace has emerged as an imperative pursuit, offering a glimmer of hope in resolving disputes and averting further hostilities. Central to this endeavor is peace agreements, carefully crafted diplomatic instruments aimed at forging conciliation and fostering a climate of tranquility. Despite being borne out of the noblest intentions, peace accords often find themselves ensnared in a labyrinth of complexities and challenges, leading to outcomes that fall short of achieving enduring peace.

The profound need for peace agreements is undeniably rooted in the dire consequences of armed conflicts. From the ancient battlefields of antiquity to the modern theaters of war, the toll of war on human lives, infrastructure, and societal fabric has been grievous. The profound suffering and loss accompanying conflicts underscore the urgency to seek alternatives that can bring harmony and stability.

To this end, peace agreements have emerged as a diplomatic tool par excellence, offering a structured framework for parties to engage in dialogue, negotiate terms, and chart a path toward reconciliation. The drafting and ratification of these agreements represent a commitment to find common ground and transcend the adversarial dynamics of armed confrontations. They embody aspirations for lasting peace, laying the foundation for mutual respect, cooperation, and the preservation of human dignity.

However, the road to enduring peace is fraught with challenges, and peace agreements are not immune to the complexities of conflict resolution. Many historical and contemporary instances have demonstrated the limitations and vulnerabilities of these diplomatic instruments. Despite the best of intentions, some peace accords have faltered, leading to renewed hostilities and dashed hopes for a stable future as a result of the following reasons:

I. Historical Perspectives on Failed Peace Agreements

Throughout history, we can identify numerous examples of peace agreements that eventually faltered, leading to the resurgence of conflicts. One such prominent case is the Treaty of Versailles following World War I. Although intended to bring lasting peace to Europe, the treaty's punitive measures against Germany sowed the seeds for future tensions, culminating in World War II. Similarly, the Camp David Accords of 1978, aimed at resolving the Israeli-Palestinian conflict, faced setbacks due to complex territorial disputes and differing interpretations of the accord's provisions. By analyzing such historical precedents, we can gain valuable insights into the factors that impede successful peace agreements.

II. Complexity of Conflicts and Stakeholder Interests

One of the primary challenges peace agreements face lies in the complexity of conflicts themselves. Armed conflicts often involve deeply entrenched grievances, historical animosities, and multifaceted political, religious, and ethnic dimensions. Attempting to address these intricate issues through simplified solutions may lead to superficial resolutions that fail to address the root causes of conflict. Additionally, the interests of various stakeholders involved in the conflict may diverge significantly, making it challenging to find common ground and reach a comprehensive agreement.

III. Lack of Inclusivity and Representation

The success of a peace agreement is often contingent on the inclusion and representation of all relevant parties in the negotiation process. The lack of confidence and legitimacy in the final accord might result from the exclusion of some factions or marginalized groups.

This exclusionary approach may also create disillusionment among those not adequately represented, leading to further conflict escalation. Ensuring the participation of diverse voices and perspectives is crucial in fostering an inclusive and durable peace agreement.

IV. Failure to Address Root Causes and Structural Issues

Peace agreements that merely address the symptoms of a conflict without tackling its underlying causes are prone to failure. Root causes often encompass economic disparities, governance challenges, and systemic inequalities. Neglecting to address these structural issues can lead to simmering discontent, providing fertile ground for future conflicts to arise. Sustainable peace requires comprehensive efforts to address the root causes and work toward societal transformation.

V. Weak Enforcement Mechanisms

Even when peace agreements are reached, weak enforcement mechanisms can jeopardize their successful implementation. Some accords lack clear frameworks for monitoring and enforcing compliance, leaving room for parties to renege on their commitments without consequence. Strong, impartial enforcement mechanisms are vital to holding parties accountable and ensuring the agreement's longevity.

VI. External Interference and Geostrategic Considerations

External interference from other nations or vested interests can undermine the prospects of a successful peace agreement. In some cases, powerful countries may have geopolitical motivations that diverge from the interests of those directly involved in the conflict. Such interference can perpetuate instability and prevent genuine and sustainable peace.

VII. Psychological Barriers and Societal Trauma

War and conflict inflict profound psychological wounds on individuals and societies. Deep-rooted trauma and animosity can create psychological barriers that hinder the reconciliation process and make trust-building a formidable challenge. Healing societal wounds and fostering empathy among adversaries are prerequisites for successful peace agreements.

VIII. Economic Incentives for Conflict

Regrettably, some groups and individuals may benefit economically from perpetuating conflict. The illicit trade of natural resources, arms, and human trafficking can create perverse incentives for continuing hostilities. Addressing economic motivations for conflict and establishing viable alternatives can help dismantle the drivers of violence.

IX. The Cost of War and Humanitarian Consequences

The human and economic costs of war are immeasurable. Armed conflicts devastate entire communities, displace populations, and disrupt essential services like healthcare and education. The humanitarian consequences of war underscore the urgency for nations to prioritize peaceful resolutions, protecting the lives and well-being of their citizens.

In light of the above factors, it becomes evident that nations must embrace peace as a strategic imperative instead of resorting to war. Pursuing peace demands the recognition of the complexity of conflicts, genuine inclusivity, addressing root causes, and enforcing agreements effectively. By opting for peace, nations can promote stability, development, and cooperation, creating a world where the prosperity and well-being of all humanity can thrive. In overcoming the challenges posed by failed peace agreements, the path to a more harmonious and peaceful future emerges, offering hope for a world free from the scourge of war.

HISTORICAL AND CONTEMPORARY CASE STUDIES OF UNSUCCESSFUL ACCORDS

Throughout history and more recently, the world has witnessed numerous attempts to achieve peace through formal agreements and accords. These diplomatic endeavors, born out of a genuine desire to end hostilities and promote stability, have aimed to address conflicts ranging from territorial disputes to ideological differences. While some peace agreements have brought about lasting tranquility, others have faced significant challenges, ultimately proving unsuccessful in their quest for peace.

Let us examine historical and contemporary case studies of unsuccessful accords and the reasons for their failure.

1. **The Treaty of Versailles (1919):**
   Following the devastation of World War I, the Treaty of Versailles was crafted to establish lasting peace in Europe. The accord sought to hold Germany accountable for the war and imposed harsh penalties, including territorial losses and reparations. However, the treaty's punitive measures sowed discontent among the German populace, fueling nationalist sentiments and setting the stage for Adolf Hitler's rise to power. World War II broke out as a result of the treaty's failure to address the fundamental political and economic causes of the conflict, highlighting the necessity of comprehensive and equitable conflict settlement.

2. **The Oslo Accords (1993):**
   The Oslo Accords, brokered between Israel and the Palestine Liberation Organization (PLO), aimed to resolve the Israeli-Palestinian conflict by outlining a roadmap for peace and Palestinian self-governance. Despite early optimism, the accords faced significant obstacles, including disagreements over Jerusalem's status, the right of Palestinian refugees to return, and the expansion

of Israeli settlements in the occupied territories. The 1995 killing of Israeli Prime Minister Yitzhak Rabin and the ensuing war weakened confidence between the parties and made it more difficult to put the agreement's principles into practice, together with these outstanding problems.

As a result, the peace process stagnated, leading to ongoing tensions and a lack of progress toward lasting peace.

3. **The Dayton Agreement (1995):**
   The Dayton Agreement ended the Bosnian War, which resulted in ethnic cleansing and mass atrocities. The accord sought to create a decentralized state structure, sharing power among Bosnia's three main ethnic groups: Bosniaks, Serbs, and Croats. However, while ending the overt hostilities, the agreement's complex system of governance failed to address deep-rooted ethnic divisions and unresolved grievances. Consequently, Bosnia and Herzegovina remains politically and ethnically divided, with the state's institutions paralyzed by persistent ethnic tensions.

4. **The Geneva II Conference (2014):**
   The Geneva II Conference aimed to find a political resolution to the Syrian civil war, which resulted in a protracted and devastating conflict. While representatives from the Syrian government and opposition factions participated, the talks quickly stalled due to fundamental disagreements over the role of President Bashar al-Assad in the transitional government and the future governance of Syria. The failure of the conference to make significant progress highlighted the complexities of finding a viable solution in the face of entrenched positions and diverging interests of regional and international actors.

5. **The Minsk Agreements (2014-2015):**
   The Minsk Agreements sought to end the armed conflict between Ukraine and Russian-backed separatists in the Donetsk and Luhansk regions. Despite several rounds of negotiations, the agreements have faced repeated violations and a lack of genuine commitment from both sides. Disagreements over implementing the accords' provisions, such as the withdrawal of heavy weaponry and local elections, have perpetuated the conflict, resulting in a protracted stalemate and continued suffering for civilians in the affected regions.

6. **The Colombian Peace Process (2016):**
   The Revolutionary Armed Forces of Colombia (FARC) and the Colombian government have been in a protracted battle for many years.

   Initially rejected in a national referendum, the peace agreement underwent revisions and was eventually ratified by the Colombian Congress. However, challenges arose during the implementation phase, including the reintegration of former FARC combatants into society, land restitution, and the rise of armed groups filling the power vacuum left by the FARC's demobilization. The imperfect implementation of the accord has led to ongoing violence in certain regions of Colombia, revealing the complexities of post-conflict transitions.

7. **The Doha Agreement (2020):**
   The Doha Agreement, brokered by the United States, aimed to facilitate a withdrawal of foreign troops from Afghanistan and pave the way for intra-Afghan peace talks. While the agreement partially reduced violence and initiated talks between the Afghan government and the Taliban, progress has been slow and hampered by continued violence and disagreements over fundamental issues. The

withdrawal of foreign troops has also led to increased territorial gains by the Taliban, creating uncertainties about the future stability of Afghanistan.

The historical and contemporary case studies of unsuccessful peace agreements underscore the intricate nature of conflict resolution and the challenges faced in establishing lasting peace. These examples reveal that addressing the root causes of conflicts, inclusivity in negotiations, comprehensive implementation strategies, and robust enforcement mechanisms are crucial elements for the success of peace agreements. The complexities of conflicts demand a nuanced approach that considers historical grievances, underlying structural issues, and the aspirations of all parties involved. While the road to peace is fraught with difficulties, the lessons learned from these case studies can guide future efforts, encouraging nations to pursue peaceful resolutions that foster stability, cooperation, and prosperity for all humanity. Only through earnest commitment and a multifaceted approach can the world hope to overcome the pitfalls that have marred past peace accords and pave the way for a more harmonious future.

THE ROLE OF SPOILERS AND VESTED INTERESTS IN DERAILING PEACE PROCESSES

Across the annals of human history, from ancient civilizations to the modern era, the world has been a stage for countless endeavors to achieve peace through formal agreements and accords. These diplomatic endeavors, borne out of a genuine and impassioned desire to end hostilities, alleviate suffering, and promote stability, have sought to address a diverse array of conflicts spanning the entire spectrum of human discord. From territorial disputes and ethnic tensions to ideological differences and ideological schisms, the pursuit of peace has been an indelible thread woven into the fabric of human civilization.

Peace agreements, as the tangible embodiment of hope and cooperation, have stood as beacons of possibility in even the darkest chapters of human history. They represent the collective aspirations of nations, leaders, and communities to rise above the tumult of war, guided by the unyielding belief in the transformative power of dialogue, empathy, and compromise. Within these meticulously drafted texts and formalized treaties, nations have endeavored to transcend the adversarial shackles of conflict and embrace the prospect of coexistence and prosperity.

Peace agreements that have been effectively implemented have led to transformative results, as demonstrated by notable examples like the peaceful negotiations led by Nelson Mandela that ended apartheid in South Africa and the dismantling of the Berlin Wall, symbolizing the reunification of Germany after years of division. These instances serve as beacons of hope, illuminating the potential that lies within the careful curation of dialogue and negotiation, which can dismantle physical and ideological barriers to pave the way for enduring peace.

However, amid these inspiring successes, history bears witness to many peace agreements that have faltered in their mission to establish lasting tranquility. Despite the best intentions of negotiators and signatories, some of these accords have encountered unforeseen challenges, insurmountable obstacles, and a plethora of complexities that have proven detrimental to their ultimate objective - the attainment of peace.

In dissecting the reasons behind the failures of such agreements, it becomes apparent that the path to lasting peace is far from straightforward. Conflicts, by their very nature, are deeply rooted in historical grievances, power dynamics, and interwoven interests that transcend the mere resolution of surface-level disputes. The involvement of multiple stakeholders further compounds the complexity of conflicts, each pursuing their agendas, making it increasingly difficult to reconcile diverging objectives and arrive at a mutually agreeable settlement.

Additionally, the efficacy of peace agreements often hinges on the inclusivity of the negotiation process, ensuring that all relevant parties are given a seat at the table. The omission of critical stakeholders or marginalized groups from the dialogue can undermine the legitimacy of the accord and result in festering grievances that linger, potentially leading to the resumption of hostilities.

Moreover, the successful implementation of peace agreements relies heavily on robust enforcement mechanisms that hold all parties accountable for their commitments. Weak or absent monitoring and enforcement can breed a climate of impunity, encouraging parties to deviate from the agreed-upon terms, thereby jeopardizing the credibility of the agreement and engendering a sense of distrust among its signatories.

Furthermore, the influence of external actors in the peace process and the broader geopolitical landscape can profoundly impact the success of peace agreements. Powerful nations or interest groups may have vested interests that diverge from the aspirations of those directly involved in the conflict, leading to undue interference and undermining the pursuit of genuine and lasting peace.

Beyond spoilers, vested interests play a crucial role in shaping the dynamics of peace processes. External actors, such as neighboring countries, international organizations, or powerful states, may harbor strategic, economic, or geopolitical interests in the conflict region. These interests can range from securing access to resources, influencing regional power dynamics, or maintaining a strategic foothold.

In some cases, these external actors may support particular parties to the conflict, either overtly or covertly, providing them with resources, arms, or diplomatic backing. Such support can empower certain factions, intensify hostilities, and undermine efforts to foster an impartial and balanced peace process.

Economic interests, particularly in resource-rich conflict zones, can also act as a driver for vested interests and spoilers. Natural resources, such as oil, minerals, or timber, can become lucrative commodities fueling conflict as armed groups or unscrupulous actors exploit them for financial gain. Continuing conflict allows these actors to control and profit from resource extraction or illegal trade, creating disincentives for peace and stability.

Furthermore, vested interests may be intertwined with broader geopolitical rivalries. Conflict regions can become arenas for proxy struggles between powerful states seeking to expand their spheres of influence. These geopolitical maneuvers can exacerbate tensions, deepen divisions, and complicate peace negotiations, as conflicting interests vie for dominance.

The presence of spoilers and vested interests poses formidable challenges to peace processes, often obstructing the path to a negotiated settlement. The use of spoilers and external support might cause the negotiation parties to lose faith in one another, making it challenging to reach an agreement.

Persistent violence and acts of terror may intimidate participants, undermining their willingness to engage in meaningful dialogue or make concessions.

Furthermore, spoilers and vested interests can erode the credibility and legitimacy of peace processes in the eyes of the affected population. As civilians witness ongoing violence and external interference, they may lose faith in the prospect of a peaceful resolution, exacerbating societal divisions and perpetuating the cycle of conflict.

Effectively countering spoilers and vested interests requires a multifaceted and adaptive approach. Some strategies to mitigate their impact include:

- Inclusive Negotiations: Ensuring that all relevant parties have a seat at the negotiating table can reduce the potential for spoilers to exploit exclusion and garner support among marginalized groups.

- Robust Enforcement Mechanisms: Establishing credible mechanisms for monitoring and enforcing the implementation of agreements can deter spoilers from violating the terms of the peace deal.

- Diplomatic Engagement: Engaging with external actors and vested interests through diplomatic channels can encourage cooperation and commitment to the peace process.

- Addressing Root Causes: Addressing the underlying grievances that fuel conflict can reduce the appeal of spoilers and create an environment more conducive to lasting peace.

- Engaging Civil Society: Civil society organizations play a vital role in advocating for peace and countering the influence of spoilers, thereby bolstering public support for the peace process.

The role of spoilers and vested interests in derailing peace processes is a challenging and ever-present reality in the pursuit of lasting peace. Armed militant groups, internal divisions, external actors, and economic interests all wield significant influence, contributing to the complexities of conflict resolution. The disruptive tactics employed by spoilers, coupled with the support they receive, can erode trust and undermine the prospects of successful negotiations. Persistent violence and acts of terror may intimidate participants, undermining their willingness to engage in meaningful dialogue or make concessions.

LEARNING FROM FAILURES TO IMPROVE FUTURE PEACE NEGOTIATIONS

Formal peace negotiations and agreements have been instrumental in resolving conflicts and forging pathways toward coexistence and stability. However, the journey toward peace is fraught with challenges, and history has witnessed its fair share of failed peace negotiations and agreements. While such failures can be disheartening, they offer invaluable lessons that, when heeded, can serve as stepping stones towards more effective and enduring peacebuilding efforts.

Understanding the Root Causes of Failure

The first step in learning from failed peace negotiations is a comprehensive understanding of the underlying reasons for their collapse. Conflicts are intricate and multifaceted, often rooted in historical grievances, power imbalances, or deeply entrenched ideological divisions. By analyzing the factors that led to the breakdown of previous negotiations, policymakers and mediators can gain insights into the challenges that must be addressed in future peace processes.

- **Inclusivity and Representation:**
  One of the critical lessons from past failures is the significance of inclusivity in peace negotiations. Excluding key stakeholders, marginalized groups, or factions with genuine grievances can undermine the legitimacy of the process and fuel resentment. Ensuring that all relevant parties have a seat at the negotiating table fosters a sense of ownership and accountability, laying the groundwork for more sustainable and widely accepted agreements.

- **Comprehensive and Contextual Solutions:**
  Peace negotiations must address conflicts' root causes and complex dynamics rather than merely addressing their surface manifestations. Superficial resolutions that fail to tackle underlying grievances are unlikely to withstand the test of time. Crafting comprehensive solutions encompassing the conflict's political, social, economic,

and cultural dimensions is crucial for creating a more stable and enduring peace.

- **Building Trust and Confidence-Building Measures:**
  Trust is a fragile commodity in conflict-ridden settings, and building confidence between parties is an essential prerequisite for successful negotiations. Confidence-building measures, such as ceasefires, prisoner exchanges, and humanitarian gestures, can create an atmosphere of goodwill and pave the way for more constructive dialogue.

- **Flexible and Adaptive Approaches:**
  Rigidity in negotiation strategies can hinder progress and alienate parties with diverse interests. Learning from past failures requires flexibility and adaptability, recognizing that peace negotiations are often fluid and subject to unforeseen challenges. Mediators and negotiators must be willing to adjust their strategies in response to changing circumstances and emerging opportunities for progress.

- **Addressing Spoilers and Vested Interests:**
  Spoilers and vested interests, both internal and external, can have a detrimental impact on peace negotiations. Understanding the motivations and tactics of these actors is essential in developing strategies to neutralize their disruptive influence. Countering spoilers requires diplomatic engagement, enforcement mechanisms, and addressing the root causes of their grievances.

- **Empowering Civil Society:**
  Civil society is essential to maintaining peace and can link communities and the parties engaged in negotiations. Peace negotiations may gain from a wider range of viewpoints and encourage more accountability to the interests of impacted communities by empowering civil society groups and supporting their meaningful involvement.

- **Timing and Sequencing:**
  The timing and sequencing of peace negotiations can significantly influence their success. Premature or ill-timed negotiations may lack the conditions for progress, while delay in engaging in dialogue may allow tensions to escalate further. Learning from past failures calls for strategic planning and careful consideration of the timing and sequencing of peace talks.

- **The Role of International Mediation:**
  International mediation can be vital in facilitating peace negotiations, providing neutral ground and expertise in conflict resolution. However, learning from previous experiences also highlights the importance of tailoring mediation efforts to the specific context of the conflict and avoiding undue interference that may undermine the ownership and legitimacy of the peace process.

- **Long-Term Commitment:**
  Peace negotiations are seldom quick fixes, and sustainable peace requires a long-term commitment from all parties involved. Learning from failures underscores the need for sustained engagement, support, and follow-through on implementing agreements.

- **Learning from Success Stories:**
  While learning from failed peace negotiations is crucial, drawing insights from successful peace processes is equally important. Analyzing the factors that contributed to successful resolutions can provide valuable guidance for future negotiations and highlight effective approaches to conflict resolution. The quest for peace and successful peace negotiations are at the heart of humanity's aspirations for a harmonious and stable world. While failures in peace processes can be disheartening, they offer invaluable opportunities for learning and growth.

CHAPTER 6

ENHANCING PEACE

In the vast tapestry of human existence, the pursuit of peace has emerged as an ever-cherished ideal, a beacon of hope amidst the dark shadows of conflict. The age-old adage "peace, not war" resonates through the annals of time, urging nations and territories to transcend the destructive tendencies of armed confrontations. Instead, the clarion call for enhancing peace echoes, beckoning societies to embrace the transformative power of cooperation and diplomacy. In a world where the consequences of conflicts are measured not merely in terms of lives lost but also in shattered economies and ravaged landscapes, the imperative to seek bilateral and multilateral agreements for economic growth, peace, stability, and security takes center stage.

This chapter delves into the significance of fostering an environment of amicable collaboration and negotiation, where the pursuit of prosperity and harmony supersedes the futile pursuit of destruction. By exploring the manifold advantages of enhancing peace, we unveil the potential of nations uniting as partners in progress, laying the foundation for a brighter, more secure future for future generations.

PEACE, AN ALTERNATIVE TO WAR

As the world continues to navigate a complex global landscape, the significance of peace as a preferable alternative to war becomes increasingly evident. The devastating consequences of armed conflicts - loss of lives, destruction of economies, and societal fractures - are solemn reminders of the futility of violence in resolving disputes.

Amidst such dire consequences, the call for nations to embrace peace, cooperation, and diplomacy gains resonance. The path of peace offers a transformative approach where bilateral and multilateral agreements become the foundation for economic growth, stability, and security. This discussion explores the multifaceted significance of peace as a powerful and viable choice and delves into the manifold advantages of embracing diplomacy to create a world where prosperity, harmony, and progress flourish.

At the core of any conflict lies the immense human cost. Wars inflict immeasurable suffering, leaving behind a trail of shattered lives and broken families. The toll on soldiers and civilians alike is indescribable, as the scars of physical and emotional trauma linger for generations. The loss of loved ones, displacement, and the agony of witnessing violence take their toll on the human spirit, leaving lasting wounds that can be hard to heal.

Economically, armed conflicts bring profound disruptions. The destruction of critical infrastructure, disruption of trade, and diversion of resources toward war efforts have severe economic consequences. The toll on businesses, investment, and employment prospects undermines growth and prosperity. The economic aftermath of war is often felt for years, hindering development and diverting funds away from crucial social and developmental programs.

Socially, war fractures the fabric of societies. Deep-rooted animosities and ethnic tensions can be further exacerbated during conflicts, leading to long-lasting divisions and challenges in fostering reconciliation. The healing process and rebuilding trust within fractured communities can be a painstaking journey, further delaying the path to sustainable peace.

In addition to the human, economic, and social costs, wars have an unfortunate tendency to perpetuate themselves. The cycle of violence can become self-perpetuating as retaliatory actions breed further retaliation, creating an ever-escalating spiral of hostility. Breaking free from this vicious cycle demands immense courage, vision, and a willingness to embrace peace as the ultimate solution to the conflict.

In stark contrast to war, diplomacy, and peaceful negotiations offer a more hopeful path. Bilateral and multilateral agreements, forged through dialogue and compromise, have the potential to yield transformative outcomes. Nations may communicate their concerns through diplomacy, establish common ground, and work toward solutions that benefit both parties. It provides a platform for understanding, empathy, and cooperation, fostering a sense of shared responsibility for global challenges.

Embracing peaceful cooperation opens doors to economic growth and stability. Nations that invest in diplomacy can foster an environment conducive to trade, investment, and economic partnerships. They can address shared challenges such as poverty, climate change, and pandemics through collaboration. Such joint efforts not only benefit individual nations but also strengthen the global economy as a whole.

Moreover, diplomatic efforts can foster trust and strengthen regional cooperation. By addressing historical grievances and finding common ground, nations can build relationships based on mutual respect and understanding. Regional cooperation can create a web of interconnectedness, where nations collaborate on security, trade, and development, ultimately contributing to a more stable and prosperous region.

In the aftermath of conflicts, diplomatic efforts play a pivotal role in humanitarian assistance and peacebuilding. Through negotiated ceasefires and peace accords, space is created for humanitarian organizations to provide aid and support to affected communities. Diplomacy can facilitate the process of post-conflict reconstruction, helping societies transition from war to peace.

International organizations are essential for fostering peace and settling disputes. Organizations like the United Nations, regional associations, and NGOs act as unbiased mediators to unite the parties and find solutions.

They provide a platform for dialogue, peacekeeping efforts, and post-conflict reconstruction.

Yet, embracing peace is not the sole responsibility of governments and political leaders. It is a collective effort that requires the commitment of global citizens. Individuals, civil society, and grassroots movements play a vital role in advocating for peaceful resolutions, raising awareness about the devastating consequences of war, and urging governments to prioritize diplomacy over armed conflict.

The choice between peace and war is a defining moment in the grand narrative of human history. Conflicts' devastating human, economic, and social costs underscore the urgency of embracing diplomacy and cooperation. Bilateral and multilateral agreements offer transformative potential, empowering nations to work together for economic growth, peace, stability, and security. Through the power of diplomacy, humanity can pave a path toward a brighter future, one where the pursuit of peace supersedes the futile pursuit of destruction.

Embracing peace is not a sign of weakness; it is a testament to the strength of our collective humanity and our determination to build a better world for generations to come. By choosing peace over war, nations can forge a path toward prosperity, stability, and security, where the collective dreams of humanity can thrive and flourish.

INCLUSIVITY AND REPRESENTATION IN PEACE NEGOTIATIONS

In the complex arena of peace negotiations, the transformative power of inclusivity and representation stands as a guiding light, illuminating the path toward lasting and sustainable peace. Successful peace processes necessitate the engagement of all relevant stakeholders, providing them with a seat at the table to ensure their voices are heard and respected. Inclusive negotiations go beyond mere participation; they empower marginalized groups and address historical grievances, fostering an environment of trust and genuine compromise. Representation also plays a crucial role, acting as a catalyst for constructive dialogue and garnering support and trust from constituencies.

The Power of Inclusivity and Representation in Peace Negotiations and as Catalysts for Constructive Dialogue

One of the primary tenets of successful peace negotiations is inclusivity. Engaging all relevant parties - governments, armed groups, civil society organizations, and marginalized communities - brings depth and legitimacy to the negotiation process. The exclusion of key stakeholders risks perpetuating underlying grievances and inhibiting the exploration of comprehensive solutions. Inclusivity also involves empowering marginalized and vulnerable groups, ensuring their voices are amplified and their rights protected. By recognizing diverse communities' unique perspectives and needs, inclusivity addresses the root causes of conflicts, fostering an environment of understanding and empathy.

Representation complements inclusivity by ensuring that diverse perspectives are at the negotiation table. Meaningful representation fosters an environment of trust and respect, creating the foundation for constructive dialogue and genuine compromise. When all parties see themselves reflected in the negotiation process, they are more likely to invest in finding common ground and sustainable solutions. Representative negotiating teams become effective conduits for communicating progress and outcomes, solidifying the legitimacy and acceptance of the peace agreement.

However, embracing inclusivity and representation in peace negotiations is not without challenges. Protracted conflicts can give rise to deep-seated animosities and distrust, hindering efforts to bring all parties to the table. Armed groups may resist participating in negotiations or engage in fragmented representations, complicating the process. Additionally, the inclusion of marginalized communities, such as women, ethnic minorities, and indigenous groups, can face cultural and systemic barriers. Gender norms, discriminatory practices, and unequal power dynamics often marginalize these groups, depriving them of meaningful representation.

The international community's role in promoting and supporting inclusivity and representation in peace negotiations is pivotal. Entities such as the United Nations and regional organizations can serve as impartial mediators, urging all parties to embrace inclusivity in their negotiation processes. International stakeholders can provide technical assistance, capacity-building, and financial support to enhance the participation of marginalized groups. Moreover, they can apply diplomatic pressure to encourage the warring parties to prioritize inclusivity and representation to achieve peace.

While international support is vital, genuine and lasting inclusivity and representation must be grounded in local ownership and empowerment. Communities affected by conflict must be actively engaged in shaping the negotiation process, with their perspectives informing the agenda and outcomes. Empowering local actors, including civil society organizations and community leaders, enables them to be more active in peace negotiations. Local initiatives for dialogue and reconciliation can complement formal negotiation processes, fostering a bottom-up approach to peacebuilding.

The transformative impact of women's inclusion in peace negotiations has been well-documented. Women bring unique perspectives, priorities, and experiences to the table, enriching the dialogue and expanding the range of potential solutions. Moreover, research has shown that peace agreements are more likely to succeed and sustain when women participate in their design and implementation. Women's inclusion fosters a greater focus on social issues, such as education, healthcare, and community development, which are vital for post-conflict recovery.

One of the primary benefits of embracing inclusivity and representation in peace negotiations is building trust among conflicting parties. By providing a forum for open dialogue and acknowledging historical grievances, peace negotiations pave the way for reconciliation. When parties see themselves reflected in the negotiation process, they are more likely to perceive it as fair and just, increasing their willingness to compromise and find common ground. This can break down barriers of distrust and animosity, creating a foundation for sustained peace.

Inclusivity and representation are crucial in active conflict situations and can serve as a preventative measure against future conflicts. By engaging all stakeholders and addressing underlying grievances, nations can proactively address the root causes of potential conflicts. Engaging diverse perspectives and marginalized communities in decision-making can foster a more inclusive and equitable society, reducing the likelihood of social unrest and grievances that fuel violence.

Measuring the success of inclusivity and representation in peace negotiations is a complex endeavor. While the inclusion of diverse perspectives is a critical step, true success lies in the implementation of agreed-upon provisions and the sustainability of peace in the long term. The success of inclusivity can be measured through the meaningful participation of all stakeholders in the negotiation process and their engagement in post-conflict reconstruction efforts. The representation can be gauged by the extent to which the negotiated agreement reflects the interests and needs of diverse groups.

Inclusivity and representation in peace negotiations hold the promise of sustainable peace that transcends the immediate resolution of conflicts and seeks to address their root causes. When all parties have a stake in the outcome and feel ownership over the negotiated agreement, there is a greater commitment to its implementation and adherence. By embracing inclusivity and representation, nations and communities can overcome divisions and build bridges toward a shared future. This approach acknowledges the interconnectedness of societies, emphasizing the imperative for collaborative efforts in achieving peace.

Inclusivity and representation in peace negotiations are essential cornerstones in pursuing lasting peace. By embracing diverse perspectives, engaging all stakeholders, and empowering marginalized communities, nations can forge a path toward genuine reconciliation and sustainable solutions. The international and local communities must wholeheartedly embrace these factors, recognizing their transformative power in fostering a world where peace thrives, and conflicts find a resolution. Inclusivity and representation are not merely lofty ideals but practical imperatives guiding humanity toward a more inclusive, just, and peaceful future. By engaging all voices and respecting the rights and needs of diverse communities, humanity can pave the way for a more equitable and harmonious world.

ADDRESSING UNDERLYING CAUSES OF CONFLICT, SUCH AS INEQUALITY AND RESOURCE DISPUTES

Across the ages, the persistent specter of conflict has loomed, darkening the paths of societies and nations alike. While the outward manifestations of conflicts may differ, a deeper analysis reveals the prevalent threads of inequality and resource disputes as their underlying origins. These fundamental causes act as rich soil, nurturing grievances and animosities, inevitably leading to eruptions of violence and upheaval. Within this complex terrain, comprehending these foundational factors becomes imperative as we strive toward a future adorned with enduring peace and harmonious coexistence.

Inequality: A Breeding Ground for Discontent

Economic and social inequality serves as a potent catalyst for conflict. The stark disparities in wealth, access to opportunities, and basic services breed discontent and resentment within marginalized communities. When a substantial portion of the population is left behind in pursuing progress and prosperity, the seeds of conflict are sown.

Economic inequality, in particular, can lead to hopelessness and alienation among the less privileged. As the wealthy elite amass wealth and influence, those struggling to make ends meet may perceive the system as rigged against them, fostering feelings of injustice and frustration.

Moreover, social inequality, such as discrimination based on race, ethnicity, or gender, perpetuates divisions and erodes societal cohesion. When certain groups face systemic prejudice and exclusion, their aspirations for dignity and equality may become intertwined with struggles for social justice, further fueling conflicts.

Resource Disputes: Fighting for Scarce Commodities

Resource disputes have been at the heart of numerous conflicts throughout history. Scarce and valuable resources, such as oil, minerals, water, and arable land, can become flashpoints for territorial disputes and economic rivalries. The competition for control over these resources can escalate tensions and trigger violent confrontations.

Resource-rich regions are often prone to exploitation and external interference as powerful nations seek to secure their access to these coveted commodities. Pursuing resources can exacerbate existing divisions and entangle countries in protracted conflicts.

Furthermore, resource mismanagement and corruption can exacerbate the impact of resource disputes. When resources are not equitably distributed or used to benefit the broader population, it can heighten feelings of injustice and contribute to societal instability.

Ethnic and Religious Tensions: Seeds of Sectarian Strife

Ethnic and religious tensions are significant drivers of conflicts worldwide. Deep-rooted historical grievances and animosities can erupt into violent confrontations, with communities pitted against each other to protect their identity and interests.

Divisive ideologies perpetuated by extremist groups can exploit ethnic and religious fault lines to rally support and further their agendas. The manipulation of identity politics can stoke fears and perpetuate cycles of violence.

Additionally, state policies that discriminate against certain ethnic or religious groups can fuel feelings of marginalization and foster a sense of collective grievance. Addressing these root causes requires promoting inclusivity, respect for diversity, and equal treatment under the law.

Political Power Struggles: Quest for Control

Political power struggles are another critical underlying cause of conflict. Ambitious leaders vying for authority and control can instigate unrest, often manipulating social and economic grievances to rally support for their causes.

Power vacuums can emerge in countries with weak governance structures and fragile institutions, leading to political instability and heightened competition for influence. These power struggles can escalate into armed conflicts if not managed through inclusive and transparent political processes.

Historical Legacies: The Ghosts of the Past

Historical legacies of colonization, imperialism, and forced displacement continue to shape contemporary conflicts. Lingering grievances over past injustices and territorial boundaries can serve as enduring sources of tension.

Resolving historical grievances requires a reckoning with the past, acknowledging past wrongs, and finding paths toward reconciliation. Dialogue, truth and reconciliation commissions, and acknowledgment of historical injustices can pave the way for healing and peacebuilding.

The Role of External Actors: A Double-Edged Sword

External actors can play a significant role in fueling or mitigating conflicts. While international support can help stabilize conflict zones and promote peace, external interference for geopolitical gain can exacerbate conflicts.

Arms sales, military aid, and covert support to warring parties can prolong conflicts and intensify violence. On the other hand, international diplomatic efforts, mediation, and peacekeeping missions can contribute to conflict resolution and post-conflict stability.

Protracted Conflicts and the Cycle of Violence

In many cases, conflicts become protracted, with violence begetting more violence. As conflicts persist over extended periods, societal trauma deepens, and avenues for peaceful resolutions may appear increasingly remote.

Breaking the cycle of violence requires a concerted effort to build trust and foster dialogue between conflicting parties. Reaching sustainable peace may require compromise, concessions, and recognition of shared interests and objectives.

Proactive measures and comprehensive strategies are needed to address the root causes of conflict. Emphasizing inclusivity and equality in governance and decision-making processes is critical in addressing inequality and social tensions. Inclusive policies prioritizing equitable resource and opportunity distribution can help address economic disparities and reduce feelings of marginalization.

Effective resource management, transparency, and accountability are crucial to avoid resource-related conflicts. Governments must ensure that the benefits of resource wealth reach all population segments, investing in social programs and infrastructure to improve living conditions for all.

Promoting intercultural dialogue and understanding is essential in addressing ethnic and religious tensions. Efforts to foster social cohesion and promote shared identities can mitigate sectarian strife and reduce the appeal of extremist ideologies.

Furthermore, robust and transparent political institutions are necessary to prevent power struggles from escalating into violent conflicts. Strengthening democratic processes, ensuring free and fair elections, and promoting political pluralism can help manage political transitions and reduce power disputes.

Addressing historical grievances requires both recognition and reconciliation. Truth and reconciliation commissions can provide spaces for dialogue, acknowledge past wrongs, and lay the foundations for healing and social cohesion.

The role of external actors should be guided by the principles of non-interference and respect for sovereignty. International diplomatic efforts should prioritize conflict resolution and promote multilateral cooperation in addressing root causes.

In protracted conflicts, transitional justice mechanisms can promote accountability, rebuild trust, and facilitate post-conflict reconstruction. Establishing a conducive environment for lasting peace necessitates substantial and enduring investments in education, healthcare, and economic opportunities.

Unraveling the Seeds of Peace

Inequality and resource disputes are powerful root causes of conflict, shaping the destinies of nations and communities alike. Understanding the complexities of these issues and their interplay is essential in devising effective solutions that address the multifaceted challenges.

By prioritizing inclusivity, equality, and justice, societies can begin to unravel the seeds of peace. Embracing transparency, dialogue, and reconciliation is crucial in healing historical wounds and building bridges toward a shared future.

The path to peace is not without challenges, but the collective efforts of governments, international actors, and civil society can pave the way for a world where conflicts find resolution and peace prevails. The pursuit of lasting peace requires unwavering commitment, compassion, and a shared vision for a more harmonious and equitable world. Through a steadfast dedication to addressing root causes and fostering dialogue, humanity can move closer to a future defined not by the darkness of conflict but by the radiant light of peace.

IMPLEMENTING SUSTAINABLE DEVELOPMENT INITIATIVES ALONGSIDE PEACE AGREEMENTS

In the quest for a more peaceful and stable world, sustainable development initiatives have emerged as essential building blocks, complementing peace agreements in fostering enduring peace and prosperity. As conflicts continue to afflict various regions, it becomes evident that peace agreements alone may not address the root causes of strife and ensure a sustainable future. By intertwining peacebuilding efforts with comprehensive sustainable development strategies, nations can create a powerful synergy that addresses social, economic, and environmental challenges, laying the groundwork for lasting peace.

The Interplay of Peace Agreements and Sustainable Development

Peace agreements are critical for ending armed conflicts and establishing frameworks for peaceful coexistence. They often entail ceasefire arrangements, disarmament plans, power-sharing agreements, and provisions for addressing grievances. While these measures aim to bring immediate stability, they may not fully address the underlying socio-economic disparities and environmental degradation contributing to conflicts.

On the other hand, sustainable development initiatives seek to tackle these root causes by promoting social inclusion, economic opportunities, and environmental protection. Integrating these initiatives alongside peace agreements can achieve a more comprehensive and holistic approach to conflict resolution.

The Root Causes of Conflict

Conflicts often arise from poverty, inequality, lack of access to basic services, and competition over scarce resources. Sustainable development initiatives play a pivotal role in addressing these root causes. By focusing on poverty alleviation, promoting education and healthcare, and enhancing economic opportunities, nations can build more inclusive societies and reduce the potential for conflict.

Environmental degradation and resource disputes are also significant drivers of conflicts. Sustainable development initiatives that prioritize environmental protection, natural resource management, and climate resilience can mitigate these issues, contributing to the prevention of conflicts related to resources.

Social Inclusion and Reconciliation

Sustainable development initiatives prioritizing social inclusion and reconciliation can help heal the wounds of conflict and build bridges between communities. Efforts to address historical grievances, promote intercultural dialogue, and ensure equal rights for all can foster a sense of belonging and shared identity within diverse societies.

Furthermore, reconciliation programs can facilitate truth-telling, forgiveness, and healing, allowing societies to move forward from past traumas and envision a future built on mutual understanding and cooperation.

Economic Stability and Inclusive Growth

Sustainable economic development is crucial for post-conflict societies to rebuild and thrive. Peace agreements may create a conducive environment for investments and economic growth, but sustainable development initiatives are needed to ensure that the benefits reach all segments of society.

By focusing on job creation, skills development, and empowering marginalized groups, sustainable development initiatives can contribute to more equitable economic growth, reducing inequalities and the potential for future conflicts rooted in economic disparities.

Strengthening Governance and Institutions

Building effective governance structures and institutions is essential for the cohesiveness of post-conflict societies. Peace agreements may lay the groundwork for political power-sharing arrangements, but sustainable development initiatives can strengthen institutions and ensure their resilience in the face of challenges.

Transparent and accountable governance is critical for effectively implementing sustainable development projects and managing resources to benefit the broader population. By promoting good governance practices, nations can reduce corruption and increase public trust in institutions, further bolstering the prospects for lasting peace.

Environmental Sustainability and Resilience

Long-term stability depends on integrating environmental sustainability, a crucial element of sustainable development, into peacebuilding initiatives. Environmental degradation and natural resource scarcity can exacerbate conflicts, particularly in regions where competition over resources is fierce.

Sustainable development initiatives prioritizing environmental conservation, climate resilience, and sustainable resource management can alleviate resource-related tensions and promote cooperation between communities and nations.

International Cooperation and Support

Implementing sustainable development initiatives alongside peace agreements requires international cooperation and support. The international community can be crucial in providing financial assistance, technical expertise, and capacity-building to post-conflict nations.

Multilateral organizations, such as the United Nations and regional development banks, can assist in coordinating and implementing sustainable development projects, ensuring that they align with the priorities and needs of the affected communities.

Challenges and Opportunities

Implementing sustainable development initiatives alongside peace agreements is not without its challenges. Post-conflict societies often face limited resources, institutional weaknesses, and ongoing security concerns, hindering development efforts. Sustaining political will and commitment to long-term development is essential, as sustainable progress requires continuity and perseverance beyond the immediate aftermath of conflicts.

However, the opportunities presented by intertwining peacebuilding with sustainable development are immense. Nations can promote a future where peace is not just the absence of conflict but a condition of thriving and well-being for everyone by tackling the core causes of conflict and building an inclusive and resilient society.

The need for a more comprehensive approach to peacebuilding becomes evident as the world grapples with ongoing conflicts and their far-reaching consequences. By implementing sustainable development initiatives alongside peace agreements, nations can create a powerful synergy that addresses the root causes of conflicts and lays the foundation for lasting peace and prosperity.

CHAPTER 7

GLOBAL PEACE ACCORD: OUTLAWING THE USE OF WAR

In the ever-evolving landscape of global dynamics, characterized by the transition to a post-industrial, multipolar world order, and the continuous development of society, the pursuit of lasting peace stands as a paramount objective. In this effort, it is crucial to create a framework paradigm that accepts many peacebuilding strategies, stimulating fresh viewpoints and a better understanding of peace and peacebuilding's theoretical and practical objectives.

Conventionally, international relations have been predominantly preoccupied with the analysis of interstate interactions. However, the emerging discipline of peace studies sheds light on the significance of social relations in fostering a peaceful world. By encompassing various dimensions and contexts, peace studies open avenues for exploring unique pathways to achieve and expand peace, encompassing diverse perspectives and conditions under which this noble vision can be realized.

This chapter embarks on a quest to delineate the foundations of a framework for global approaches to peace. Through a comprehensive exploration of different perspectives, it aims to unravel the intricate web of interconnected elements that underpin the pursuit of peace in a world marked by complexity and diversity.

At the heart of this endeavor lies the aspiration to outlaw the use of war as a means of conflict resolution. As nations and societies grapple with the consequences of armed conflicts, the imperative to foster dialogue, understanding, and cooperation takes precedence over the destructive path of violence. The Global Peace Accord, envisioned in this framework, dauntlessly calls for the renunciation of war as a legitimate tool in settling disputes, aiming to transcend boundaries and ideologies to forge a common commitment to peace.

This visionary accord seeks to transcend the traditional boundaries of international relations and peace studies by amalgamating various disciplines and perspectives, delving into the multifaceted nature of peace, and exploring the interconnectedness of social, political, and economic factors in shaping a peaceful world.

This chapter endeavors to lay the groundwork for a comprehensive understanding of the proposed Global Peace Accord. Shedding light on the major areas of existing research offers a guiding beacon for future investigations, igniting a collective quest for a world where the echoes of war are silenced and the harmonious symphony of peace resounds. As we embark on this transformative journey, the vision of a world outlawing the use of war beckons us to embrace unity, dialogue, and cooperation as the catalysts for a brighter and more peaceful tomorrow.

ARGUMENTS FOR A GLOBAL TREATY TO PROHIBIT WAR AS A MEANS OF CONFLICT RESOLUTION

In the ever-changing landscape of global dynamics, the call for a global treaty to prohibit war as a means of conflict resolution emerges as a visionary endeavor. This transformative proposal seeks to address the complex challenges of our time by fostering an environment of peace, cooperation, and diplomacy. In this comprehensive discussion, we explore the multifaceted arguments in favor of such a treaty, backed by comprehensive research and a commitment to a more harmonious world.

At the core of the argument lies a compelling humanitarian imperative. The devastating impact of armed conflicts on civilian populations cannot be overstated. Innocent lives are lost, families are torn apart, and war violence displaces communities. By enshrining a treaty that unequivocally condemns war as a conflict resolution tool, we emphasize the value of human lives and prioritize the protection of vulnerable populations.

Beyond the humanitarian aspect, a global treaty against war aligns with the pursuit of sustainable development and progress. The exorbitant costs of military expenditures drain valuable resources that could otherwise be channeled into essential areas such as education, healthcare, and poverty alleviation. Redirecting these funds towards peaceful endeavors empowers nations to invest in their citizens' well-being, fostering greater prosperity and elevating the standard of living.

Crucially, the treaty encourages a paradigm shift towards diplomacy and peaceful conflict resolution. Instead of resorting to violence, nations are urged to engage in dialogue, negotiation, and mediation to address their differences. This approach promotes lasting solutions founded on trust, cooperation, and mutual respect. Diplomacy becomes the cornerstone of resolving disputes, and a shared commitment to peace binds the international community.

The environmental dimension of a treaty prohibiting war cannot be overlooked. Armed conflicts leave behind a trail of destruction, polluting the earth and disrupting ecosystems. Toxic chemicals, deforestation, and the devastation of natural habitats have far-reaching consequences on the planet's health. By embracing a treaty that renounces war, we pave the way for preserving our environment and promoting sustainable development.

In cultivating a culture of peace, the treaty serves as a powerful catalyst for change. It inspires nations to celebrate diversity, cultivate empathy, and embrace cooperation as a means to resolve conflicts. The treaty encourages individuals and communities to transcend borders and work together towards a shared vision of peace by fostering a sense of global citizenship.

The proposal for a global treaty to prohibit war as a means of conflict resolution is not a mere idealistic aspiration but a pragmatic and necessary step towards a more peaceful world. The arguments in support of such a treaty underscore its transformative potential, grounded in compassion, diplomacy, and a shared commitment to humanity's collective well-being. By embracing the vision of a world outlawing the use of war, we take a decisive stride towards a future where cooperation, dialogue, and understanding prevail over violence and animosity. As we navigate the complexities of the modern world, the pursuit of peace must become our shared responsibility and the foundation upon which we build a more harmonious tomorrow for generations to come.

CHALLENGES AND OBJECTIONS TO ACHIEVING A COMPREHENSIVE PEACE ACCORD

In the pursuit of lasting peace, nations, and societies encounter a myriad of challenges and objections that pose significant barriers to achieving a comprehensive peace accord. Thorough research reveals key challenges and objections that hinder the path to peace, making peace-building a complex and intricate process.

One of the primary challenges lies in deep-rooted historical grievances that fuel animosity between conflicting parties. Historical injustices, territorial disputes, and unresolved conflicts cast a long shadow over the present, making it difficult to foster trust and cooperation among parties.

Intractable conflicts characterized by deep-seated hostilities and entrenched positions present a major obstacle to peace accords. Parties are often unwilling to compromise or engage in meaningful dialogue, and the persistence of violence further complicates the peace process.

Power struggles and geopolitical interests also play a significant role in hindering peace accords. Conflicting interests among influential nations and regional powers can complicate peace negotiations, as these actors may seek to advance their strategic agendas at the expense of peace and stability.

A critical objection to many peace accords is the lack of inclusivity and representation in the negotiation process. Peace negotiations often involve a select group of elite actors, neglecting the voices and concerns of marginalized communities and minorities.

The successful implementation of disarmament, demobilization, and reintegration (DDR) programs presents significant challenges in post-conflict settings. Demobilizing and reintegrating former combatants into society requires comprehensive support and resources to ensure their successful reintegration and prevent a return to violence.

Peace processes often face opposition from spoilers and saboteurs - individuals or groups seeking to undermine or derail the peace accord for their own vested interests. Identifying and countering the actions of spoilers becomes crucial in safeguarding the progress toward peace.

Socioeconomic inequalities and grievances can fuel unrest and perpetuate cycles of conflict. Addressing socioeconomic disparities and ensuring inclusive development becomes essential in building a foundation for lasting peace.

Post-conflict settings often face security challenges and the risk of relapse into violence. Navigating the delicate balance between security and peacebuilding efforts is vital to sustaining the gains made in the peace process.

The involvement of external actors in conflict-affected regions can either support or undermine peace efforts. Striking a delicate balance between international involvement and respecting national sovereignty is essential in fostering a conducive environment for peace.

Addressing historical crimes and promoting reconciliation need transitional justice procedures such as truth-and-reconciliation commissions and accountability systems. However, implementing these processes is challenging, as it requires balancing the need for justice with the imperative of reconciliation and building a common future.

Achieving a comprehensive peace accord is challenging and complex, necessitating creative and innovative approaches to overcome these hurdles. Addressing historical grievances, embracing inclusivity, countering spoilers, and fostering a culture of peace are essential components of a successful peacebuilding strategy. As we navigate the terrain of peacebuilding, our unwavering dedication to fostering global understanding and cooperation becomes the bedrock upon which we build a world where the symphony of peace replaces the echoes of war.

THE ROLE OF INTERNATIONAL LAW AND ENFORCEMENT MECHANISMS

Undoubtedly, the devastating aftermath of war has left indelible scars on societies across the globe. The haunting images of destruction, loss, and suffering serve as poignant reminders of the human cost of armed conflicts. The pressing need for a comprehensive and inclusive approach to peace became increasingly evident in the wake of such a profound tragedy.

In response to the horrors of war, the global community recognized the urgency to establish a framework that would unequivocally outlaw the use of war as a conflict resolution. Such a framework would transcend national borders and ideologies, fostering a collective commitment to prevent and resolve conflicts through peaceful means.

The Evolution of International Law

Engaging in the rich tapestry of human history, the evolution of international law unfolds like an intricate mosaic woven with threads of ancient wisdom and modern aspirations. Tracing its roots back to the dawn of civilization, early societies recognized the importance of establishing rules to govern relations between states and individuals. From the Code of Hammurabi in ancient Mesopotamia to the Laws of Solon in ancient Athens, early legal systems laid the groundwork for the emergence of a more structured international order.

However, the cataclysmic events of the 20th century acted as a crucible, shaping international law into a force for peace and global cooperation. The devastation of two World Wars, with their immeasurable loss of life and unfathomable suffering, served as a stark wake-up call to humanity. In the aftermath of such unprecedented horror, the pressing need for a new paradigm of international relations became evident.

In 1945, the world witnessed a historic moment as the United Nations, a visionary organization, was founded to prevent future wars and promote collective security. The establishment of the UN marked a pivotal stride forward in the evolution of international law, cementing the principles of sovereignty, territorial integrity, and the peaceful resolution of disputes as its guiding pillars.

With its Charter in place, the UN became a beacon of hope, a forum where nations could come together, share their aspirations, and forge alliances for a more peaceful world. The General Assembly, as the embodiment of the collective voice of the international community, provided a platform for dialogue, cooperation, and problem-solving. The Security Council, entrusted with the responsibility of maintaining international peace and security, gained prominence as the global guardian against aggression and conflict.

The creation of specialized institutions and agencies inside the UN system significantly aided the development of international law. Notably, the United Nations Educational, Scientific, and Cultural Organization (UNESCO), the World Health Organization (WHO), and the International Labor Organization (ILO) have all made significant contributions to developing international collaboration and building a culture of global solidarity.

The expansion of international law did not end with the establishment of the UN; it continued to evolve, reflecting the changing dynamics of the world. The 1948 Universal Declaration of Human Rights passage marked a key turning point, asserting each person's intrinsic dignity and unalienable rights, regardless of race, religion, or nationality.

The adoption of several conventions and treaties in the next decades, which addressed problems like genocide, racial discrimination, and environmental protection, strengthened the position of international law in solving global problems. Treaties like the Geneva Conventions sought to safeguard the rights and protections of civilians and prisoners of war during armed conflicts.

The evolution of international law was not without its challenges, as the dynamics of power and politics sometimes influenced the implementation and enforcement of legal norms. Nevertheless, the collective resolve to create a more just and peaceful world remained strong.

Today, international law continues to adapt and respond to emerging challenges, such as cyber warfare, climate change, and terrorism. The International Criminal Court (ICC) stands as a symbol of accountability, holding individuals accountable for the most heinous crimes under international law.

The evolution of international law is an ongoing journey reflective of the aspirations and struggles of humanity. It is a testament to the power of dialogue, cooperation, and shared values in shaping a world where peace, justice, and human rights prevail. As the global community stands at the threshold of a new era, the significance of international law in building a harmonious and prosperous future cannot be overstated. It is a journey that transcends borders, ideologies, and cultures, illuminating the path toward a world where the harmonious symphony of peace silences the echoes of war.

The United Nations Charter and the Prohibition of War

The United Nations Charter serves as the bedrock of international law, enshrining the principles of sovereign equality, peaceful dispute resolution, and non-use of force in international relations. The threat or use of force against a state's political independence or territorial integrity is expressly forbidden by Article 2(4) of the Charter.

The Charter's emphasis on peaceful resolution and collective security mechanisms provides a framework for outlawing the use of war as a tool of aggression.

The Role of Customary International Law

Beyond the UN Charter, customary international law plays a vital role in outlawing war. Customary law encompasses longstanding practices and behaviors accepted as binding on states. The prohibition of war has gradually become a norm of customary international law, reinforced by the widespread rejection of aggressive wars and the acceptance of peaceful dispute resolution.

International Treaties and Agreements

International treaties and agreements form a cornerstone of international law in outlawing war. Treaties such as the Geneva Conventions and the Kellogg-Briand Pact (Pact of Paris) are pivotal in regulating armed conflicts, protecting civilians, and condemning wars of aggression. The Kellogg-Briand Pact, in particular, renounces war as an instrument of national policy, with signatories pledging to seek peaceful means to resolve disputes.

The Role of International Courts and Tribunals

International courts and tribunals guard international law, ensuring its implementation and enforcement. The International Court of Justice (ICJ) is essential in resolving disputes between countries and upholding international law's norms. Through its rulings and decisions, the International Court of Justice (ICJ) upholds the prohibition of war and promotes peaceful dispute resolution.

The Responsibility to Protect (R2P)

In international law, the idea of the Responsibility to Protect (R2P) has become essential. R2P emphasizes that the international community has a responsibility to protect individuals against crimes against humanity, including genocide, war crimes, ethnic cleansing, and genocide. R2P contributes to the ultimate goal of foregoing the use of force by preventing conflicts and resolving their root causes.

International Human Rights Law

International human rights law serves as a foundation for peacebuilding and conflict prevention. Protecting and promoting human rights are intrinsically linked to preventing conflicts and ensuring a peaceful world. Upholding human rights principles contributes to creating conditions where war is rejected to address grievances.

Enforcing International Law

The development of international law gains importance due to its dependence on enforcement mechanisms. Within the UN Charter, Chapter VII confers upon the Security Council, a crucial component of the UN, the authority to enforce sanctions and authorize using force to uphold or restore global peace and security. However, political considerations may hinder the Security Council's decision-making process, creating obstacles to effective enforcement.

Strengthening the International Criminal Court (ICC)

The International Criminal Court (ICC) is critical in holding individuals accountable for war crimes, genocide, and crimes against humanity. The ICC's jurisdiction and prosecutions deter potential perpetrators, reinforcing the prohibition of war and promoting accountability.

The Role of Civil Society and Non-Governmental Organizations (NGOs)

Civil society and NGOs have become instrumental in promoting international law and peacebuilding initiatives. Through advocacy, education, and mobilization, these organizations raise awareness, build consensus, and drive governments to commit to outlawing the use of war.

The role of international law and enforcement mechanisms in outlawing the use of war cannot be understated. As we navigate the complexities of the modern world, all stakeholders' continued engagement and creativity are vital in ensuring that international law serves as a powerful force for peace, justice, and humanity. By embracing the vision of a world without war, we reaffirm our commitment to fostering a global community where conflicts are resolved through dialogue, cooperation, and mutual respect, ultimately paving the way for a brighter and more harmonious future for all.

PROMOTING A CULTURE OF PEACE AND NON-VIOLENCE THROUGH EDUCATION AND ADVOCACY

Building a culture of peace requires a multifaceted approach beyond mere ceasefire agreements or diplomatic negotiations. Education and advocacy stand at the forefront of this transformative journey, empowering individuals and communities to embrace peaceful coexistence and resolve conflicts through non-violent means.

Education serves as a cornerstone for nurturing a culture of peace and non-violence. It is within the classroom that the seeds of compassion, empathy, and understanding are sown. By integrating peace education into curricula at all levels, from early childhood to higher education, societies can instill a deep appreciation for diversity and the importance of dialogue in their citizens. Peace education encourages critical thinking and conflict resolution skills, enabling individuals to challenge stereotypes and biases and fostering an environment conducive to peaceful interactions.

Cultivating global citizenship is at the heart of promoting a culture of peace. Education empowers individuals to recognize their interconnectedness with people around the world, promoting a sense of shared responsibility for the well-being of humanity and the planet. Through exposure to diverse cultures, histories, and perspectives, students gain the tools to navigate complex global issues, transcending borders and embracing a collective vision of peace and unity.

Advocacy is a powerful tool in promoting peace and non-violence on a broader scale. Civil society organizations, grassroots movements, and individuals can engage in advocacy efforts to raise awareness about peace-related issues, influence public opinion, and press for policy changes. Advocacy campaigns can focus on disarmament, conflict resolution, social justice, and human rights, mobilizing communities to become agents of positive change.

The media is a key factor in affecting public perception and behavior. The transmission of false information and incendiary narratives that could ignite conflict can be blocked by encouraging media literacy, critical thinking, and ethical journalism.

Societies can foster an informed and empathetic public discourse by encouraging media platforms to prioritize peace journalism, which emphasizes constructive reporting and solutions-oriented coverage.

Effective communication is essential in conflict resolution and reconciliation processes. Teaching constructive dialogue and mediation skills empowers individuals to engage in open, respectful, and empathetic conversations, even amid differing viewpoints. Mediation training equips individuals with the tools to address conflicts peacefully, paving the way for mutual understanding and reconciliation.

Promoting peace and non-violence begins at the grassroots level. Communities can establish local peace committees, conflict resolution centers, and restorative justice programs to address disputes within their neighborhoods and foster a culture of reconciliation. Engaging community leaders, religious institutions, and youth organizations can be instrumental in cultivating a culture of peace that extends beyond geographical boundaries.

Religion and faith can be powerful forces for peace when used to build bridges rather than walls. Interfaith dialogue fosters understanding, respect, and cooperation among people of different religious beliefs, strengthening social cohesion and preventing religiously motivated conflicts. Interfaith initiatives provide platforms for diverse communities to unite, celebrating their shared humanity and collective pursuit of peace.

Promoting peace and non-violence begins at the grassroots level. Communities can establish local peace committees, conflict resolution centers, and restorative justice programs to address disputes within their neighborhoods and foster a culture of reconciliation. Engaging community leaders, religious institutions, and youth organizations can be instrumental in cultivating a culture of peace that extends beyond geographical boundaries.

Empowering women and promoting gender equality are essential elements in building lasting peace. When women are involved in decision-making processes and conflict-resolution efforts, outcomes are more inclusive and sustainable. The advancement of gender equality and peace may be advanced via education that questions conventional gender roles and stereotypes.

In the aftermath of conflicts, peacebuilding efforts are critical for healing societies and preventing relapses into violence. Rehabilitation programs, trauma healing initiatives, and reconciliation processes help communities recover from the scars of war. Education, particularly peace education, plays a pivotal role in creating a sense of hope and resilience, nurturing future generations to become peacemakers.

The promotion of a culture of peace and non-violence is a crucial function of governments and international organizations. The funding of initiatives aimed at promoting peace and advocacy campaigns that support addressing the underlying causes of conflict are all options open to policymakers. The diplomatic endeavor to avert crises and promote amicable settlements is of utmost importance on a global scale.

Promoting a culture of peace and non-violence through education and advocacy is an ongoing journey that requires collective effort, determination, and creativity. By investing in education that fosters compassion, empathy, and critical thinking, societies can nurture future generations to be agents of peace. Empowering individuals to engage in advocacy and dialogue amplifies voices for positive change, driving transformation on local and global levels. By embracing the interconnectedness of humanity and recognizing the shared responsibility for a peaceful world, societies can move toward a future where conflicts are resolved through non-violent means and a culture of peace flourishes. Through this collective commitment, we lay the foundation for a world where the harmonious symphony of peace replaces the echoes of violence.

CHAPTER 8

THE ROLE OF COURTS IN CONFLICT RESOLUTION

In the wake of the catastrophic Second World War, the international community grappled with the harrowing realization that existing conflict resolution and peacekeeping mechanisms had proven inadequate. The failure of the League of Nations to prevent the outbreak of war necessitated a reimagining of global governance to ensure that such a devastating conflagration would never recur. In response, the United Nations (UN) was born with the ambitious mandate to safeguard world peace and promote international cooperation.

The International Court of Justice (ICJ), which was formed as the UN's primary judicial body, is a crucial part of the organization of the UN. The Permanent Court of International Justice of the defunct League of Nations gave birth to the International Court of Justice (ICJ), which was intended to serve as an impartial arbiter in settling disputes between governments, provide a channel for amicable resolution, and forestall the outbreak of armed war.

The foundational principles of the International Court of Justice are enshrined in the United Nations Charter, making it a vital component of the global framework for conflict resolution. By virtue of the

Charter, all UN member states are automatic signatories to the ICJ Statute, acknowledging its authority as a forum for resolving disputes peacefully. The Court's mandate, therefore, lies in adjudicating matters arising between states, facilitating dialogue, and offering legal interpretations to promote a rules-based international order.

However, while establishing the ICJ represented a significant step forward in pursuing global peace, its effectiveness has not been without limitations and challenges. One fundamental constraint lies in the voluntary nature of its jurisdiction; the Court's authority to resolve disputes between states is contingent on the parties' consent. Consequently, not all disputes between nations are brought before the ICJ for adjudication, potentially leaving significant conflicts unresolved.

Furthermore, the political dynamics within the United Nations Security Council have sometimes overshadowed the Court's impartiality and effectiveness in conflict resolution. The Council's five permanent members, armed with the power of the veto, hold considerable sway over international affairs, sometimes influencing the outcome of cases brought before the ICJ. This politicization of international law has raised concerns about the Court's ability to remain a truly neutral and independent judge.

According to this paper, resolving these concerns is critical to strengthening the role of courts, especially the International Court of Justice, in the pursuit of global peace. It is nevertheless of utmost importance to preserve the Court's impartiality while carefully juggling permissive participation and compelling jurisdiction. To develop a comprehensive and effective strategy for resolving conflicts, other peaceful dispute resolution techniques such as mediation, conciliation, and arbitration should be considered alongside litigation.

In light of the complex and ever-evolving nature of global challenges, the role of courts in conflict resolution demands constant scrutiny and adaptation. As we delve into the intricacies of the International Court of Justice's operation, we must remain cognizant of the broader context in which it operates—the pursuit of lasting peace and the advancement of international justice. Only through a holistic understanding of the Court's strengths, limitations, and potential for improvement can we pave the way for a more secure and harmonious world, where conflicts are resolved peacefully and the horrors of war relegated to the annals of history.

THE EVOLUTION AND EFFECTIVENESS OF INTERNATIONAL COURTS

The evolution and effectiveness of international courts in conflict resolution have been remarkable, contributing to preventing wars and fostering a culture of global peace. The origins of international courts can be traced back to ancient civilizations, where arbitrators and mediators were employed to settle disputes between states. However, it was not until the 20th century that the modern concept of international courts began to take shape.

Establishing the Permanent Court of International Justice (PCIJ) in 1920 under the League of Nations marked a pivotal moment in the evolution of international judicial mechanisms. Despite its limitations and eventual demise with the League of Nations, the PCIJ laid the groundwork for the creation of its successor, the International Court of Justice (ICJ).

Established in 1945 under the United Nations, the ICJ emerged as the UN's principal judicial organ, inheriting the PCIJ's legacy. Tasked with adjudicating legal disputes between states and providing advisory opinions on legal matters, the ICJ became a cornerstone of the UN's mission to promote peace, security, and human rights on a global scale.

The effectiveness of international courts in conflict resolution stems from their crucial roles:

1. **Providing a Forum for Dispute Resolution:**
   International courts offer a neutral platform for states to resolve their disputes peacefully. By providing a legal arena for parties to present their arguments, the ICJ and other international courts facilitate dialogue and negotiation, reducing the likelihood of resorting to armed conflict. The binding nature of the courts' decisions encourages states to seek diplomatic solutions, reinforcing the significance of peaceful coexistence.

2. **Upholding the Rule of Law:**
   International courts play a critical role in upholding the rule of law at the global level. Through their decisions and interpretations of international law, these courts establish precedents that guide states in their conduct and interactions. By setting clear legal boundaries and norms, international courts deter states from engaging in aggressive behavior and provide a framework for resolving disputes based on established legal principles.

3. **Promoting Peaceful Settlements:**
   International courts promote peaceful settlements by offering alternative avenues for resolving disputes. Parties to a conflict can seek legal recourse instead of resorting to military force, thereby avoiding the immense human suffering and destruction associated with armed conflicts. The existence of a judicial mechanism empowers states to address grievances through legal means, fostering a culture of peaceful resolution.

4. **Enhancing Diplomatic Relations:**
   The involvement of international courts in conflict resolution can strengthen diplomatic relations between states. The voluntary

submission to the court's jurisdiction demonstrates the parties' commitment to seeking a peaceful resolution. Engaging in the legal process can also facilitate communication and understanding between parties, improving relations and greater prospects for long-term peace.

5. **Enforcing Human Rights and Humanitarian Law:**
   International courts play a vital role in enforcing human rights and humanitarian law, ensuring accountability for violations of international norms. By holding states and individuals accountable for their actions, international courts deter future violations and promote respect for human rights and humanitarian principles. This can significantly prevent conflicts fueled by human rights abuses and foster a culture of respect for international law.

6. **Supporting Post-Conflict Reconciliation:**
   International courts can also support post-conflict reconciliation and transitional justice efforts. By addressing past atrocities and holding perpetrators accountable, these courts contribute to healing and promote justice among affected communities. This can be instrumental in rebuilding trust and stability in post-conflict societies.

However, despite their many achievements, international courts also face challenges and criticisms. Their jurisdiction is limited, relying on the parties consent, which means not all disputes are brought before the courts. Additionally, enforcement of court decisions may be challenging, especially when powerful states refuse to comply with rulings. Political considerations and pressures can also impact the courts' impartiality, potentially undermining their credibility.

The evolution and effectiveness of international courts in conflict resolution have been instrumental in preventing wars and fostering global peace. As the world continues to face complex global challenges, the evolution and effectiveness of international courts will remain critical in shaping a more harmonious and secure world where conflicts are resolved peacefully and lasting peace is embraced.

INTERNATIONAL CRIMINAL COURT (ICC) AND ITS IMPACT ON ACCOUNTABILITY

The International Criminal Court (ICC) has emerged as a critical institution in international law, striving to promote accountability and equity between conflicting states. Established by the Rome Statute in 1998 and commencing its operations in 2002, the ICC represents a monumental step towards ensuring that perpetrators of heinous crimes are held accountable, regardless of their position or status.

The ICC's Role in Accountability

The primary mandate of the ICC is to prosecute individuals responsible for genocide, war crimes, crimes against humanity, and the crime of aggression. By focusing on individuals rather than states, the ICC addresses the issue of accountability at a personal level, holding individuals accountable for their actions irrespective of their official positions or affiliations. This departure from the traditional focus on state responsibility allows the ICC to tackle impunity and deliver justice to victims who have often suffered immensely during conflicts.

One of the notable features of the ICC's accountability mechanism is its complementarity principle. According to this principle, the ICC serves as a court of last resort, intervening only when national courts are unwilling or unable to prosecute individuals for the aforementioned crimes. This approach encourages national jurisdictions to take responsibility for their criminal proceedings and promotes the idea that states are primarily responsible for ensuring accountability within their territories.

Impact on Equity between Conflicting States

The ICC's pursuit of accountability has significant implications for equity between conflicting states. When one party to a conflict commits grave crimes, the ICC's intervention helps level the playing field by providing justice for victims and deterring future abuses. This equitable approach sends a powerful message that no one is above the law and that all parties involved in conflicts must be held accountable for their actions.

Furthermore, the ICC's impartiality and independence from state influence contribute to promoting equity. Unlike ad hoc tribunals established for specific conflicts, the ICC operates as a permanent institution, ensuring consistent application of international law regardless of the nature of the conflict or the identity of the parties involved. This consistency in applying justice fosters a sense of fairness and equity, reinforcing the ICC's role as an objective arbiter of international crimes.

The ICC's Impact on International Justice

The establishment of the ICC represents a pivotal advancement in the pursuit of global justice. Ad hoc tribunals have also been formed prior to its formation to address past crimes, but with restrictions on their jurisdiction and time frames, such as the International Criminal Tribunal for the former Yugoslavia (ICTY) and the International Criminal Tribunal for Rwanda (ICTR).

In contrast, the ICC's permanent nature enables it to address crimes not only in ongoing conflicts but also those committed in the future. This forward-looking approach sends a clear and resolute message that accountability for international crimes remains an ongoing commitment, regardless of evolving conflicts and challenges. As the ICC continues to hear cases and render judgments, it reinforces the principle that justice should be unbounded by time or circumstances.

Moreover, the ICC's focus on complementarity has encouraged states to strengthen their legal systems and enhance their capacity to prosecute international crimes domestically. This capacity-building aspect of the ICC's work contributes to the broader goal of promoting the rule of law and enhancing accountability at the national level, fostering a culture of justice and human rights.

Challenges and Criticisms

Despite its significant impact on accountability and equity, the ICC faces various challenges and criticisms that impact its effectiveness:

1. **Limited Jurisdiction:** The ICC's jurisdiction is limited to crimes committed on the territory of states that are parties to the Rome Statute or by nationals of those states. As a result, the ICC cannot investigate crimes committed by individuals from non-member states, limiting its reach in certain conflicts.

2. **Political Influence:** The ICC's work can be subject to political influence, especially when powerful states are involved in conflicts. The potential for political pressure on the court or non-cooperation from states can hinder its effectiveness in pursuing accountability.

3. **Resource Constraints:** The ICC's limited resources and caseload can impact its ability to handle all cases effectively and efficiently. Given the court's workload, prioritizing cases and ensuring a timely and fair trial process can be challenging.

4. **State Cooperation:** The ICC's success heavily relies on states' cooperation in executing arrest warrants and providing access to evidence and witnesses. Non-cooperation from states can hinder the court's ability to carry out its mandate effectively.

5. **Perceived Bias:** Some critics argue that the ICC disproportionately targets African countries, leading to perceptions of bias in its

operations. This criticism has raised questions about the court's universality and handling of cases involving powerful states.

The International Criminal Court has made significant strides in promoting accountability and equity between conflicting states. Its role in prosecuting individuals for grave international crimes and its impartiality in applying justice contribute to its impact on international justice. By fostering a culture of accountability and deterring future atrocities, the ICC serves as a beacon of hope for victims of heinous crimes.

However, the court also faces challenges that must be addressed to enhance its effectiveness. Ensuring broad and fair access to justice, overcoming political influence, and addressing resource constraints are critical to strengthening the ICC's role as a global champion of accountability and equity. As the world grapples with complex conflicts and atrocities, the ICC's continued evolution and adaptability will play a pivotal role in shaping a more just and equitable world where international crimes are met with unwavering resolve and where victims find solace in pursuing justice.

LEGAL CHALLENGES IN PROSECUTING WAR CRIMES AND CRIMES AGAINST HUMANITY

In the face of horrific atrocities, it is a difficult and hard duty to defend the values of justice and accountability via the prosecution of war crimes and crimes against humanity.

One of the primary legal challenges in prosecuting war crimes and crimes against humanity is the lack of universal jurisdiction. Jurisdictional issues arise when crimes are committed across borders, and the alleged perpetrators may be outside the territory of the prosecuting state. In such cases, achieving justice becomes complicated, and this challenge can hinder the ability of national courts to prosecute offenders, necessitating the involvement of international tribunals or courts with universal jurisdiction.

Criminals who have committed war crimes and crimes against humanity may be granted immunity or amnesty, particularly if they are in positions of authority within the government. The pursuit of justice may be hampered and a culture of impunity may be maintained by granting immunity or amnesty.

Many states grant immunity to high-ranking officials, arguing that it is essential for peace and reconciliation. Balancing the need for accountability with the imperative of post-conflict stability poses a significant challenge to the legal process.

Gathering admissible and credible evidence is crucial for successful prosecutions. However, evidence collection can be extremely challenging in conflict zones due to security risks and limited access to crime scenes and witnesses. The destruction or manipulation of evidence by the perpetrators further complicates the process. Overcoming these obstacles requires establishing secure mechanisms for evidence collection and preservation and protecting witnesses and victims.

Witness protection is critical to prosecuting war crimes and crimes against humanity. Witnesses often fear retaliation and may be unwilling to testify, making it challenging to build a strong case. Protecting the integrity of the justice system and encouraging victims to come forward and provide their testimony requires witness protection and collaboration. To deal with this issue, international courts and tribunals frequently implement stringent protection measures.

Establishing command responsibility and the chain of command can be complex, especially in cases where crimes are committed in the context of armed conflicts involving multiple actors. Holding commanders accountable for crimes committed by their subordinates requires establishing a direct link between the superior's orders and the commission of the crimes. Overcoming this challenge involves thorough investigations and access to credible evidence of superior responsibility.

Political interference can significantly impact the prosecution of war crimes and crimes against humanity. Powerful states may exert pressure on national authorities or international bodies to impede or halt investigations and prosecutions involving their nationals or allies. Additionally, diplomatic immunity can shield high-ranking officials from prosecution, making it difficult to hold them accountable for their actions. Addressing these challenges requires maintaining the independence and impartiality of judicial processes and ensuring that political considerations do not hinder the pursuit of justice.

The statute of limitations can be a major barrier to the prosecution of war crimes and crimes against humanity, particularly when a lot of time has passed since the crimes were committed.

In many jurisdictions, the statute of limitations can prevent prosecutions after a certain period, limiting accountability for past atrocities. Addressing this challenge may involve extending or abolishing statutes of limitations for certain heinous crimes.

Jurisdictional conflicts may arise when multiple states or international tribunals claim jurisdiction over the same crimes or perpetrators. This can lead to legal complexities and delays in the prosecution process. Establishing clear guidelines for jurisdiction and coordination between different jurisdictions can help mitigate this challenge.

The extradition of suspects to face trial in the prosecuting state or international tribunal can be challenging, especially when suspects are located in countries that lack extradition treaties or have conflicting legal systems. Enforcement of arrest warrants can also be problematic, particularly when suspects are in territories beyond the reach of the prosecuting authorities. International cooperation and diplomatic efforts are essential to address these challenges effectively.

Securing the political will and sufficient resources for war crimes and crimes against humanity prosecutions can be a daunting task. Legal proceedings are often expensive and time-consuming, requiring substantial financial and logistical support. A lack of political will to prioritize justice and allocate necessary resources can hamper the success of prosecutions.

The values of justice, accountability, and human rights must be upheld through prosecuting those who commit war crimes and crimes against humanity.

However, numerous legal challenges must be navigated to ensure successful prosecutions. Overcoming these obstacles requires international cooperation, political commitment, and the establishment of robust mechanisms for evidence collection, witness protection, and coordination between different jurisdictions. By addressing these challenges head-on, the international community can strengthen its resolve to combat impunity and create a world where justice prevails, victims find solace, and perpetrators are held accountable for their actions.

CHAPTER 9

INTERNATIONAL PEACE COURT

The idea of an International Peace Court arises as a glimmer of hope and an embodiment of humanity's collective desire for long-lasting tranquility in a world full of conflicts and difficulties. The International Peace Court is a radical idea in international law that aims to break down sovereign boundaries and promote a culture of peace and non-violence.

The roots of this visionary institution can be traced back to the devastating consequences of two world wars within three decades and the profound realization that the existing mechanisms for conflict resolution were insufficient to prevent such catastrophic events. In response to this urgent need for a transformative solution, the United Nations and its auxiliary, the International Court of Justice, were established to usher in an era of international security and cooperation.

However, the elusiveness of true global peace continues to be a haunting reality. The emergence of nuclear weapons, with their unfathomable potential for destruction, is a stark reminder of the ever-present threat of conflict. The limitations and challenges faced by existing international mechanisms in addressing complex conflicts have sparked a compelling call for an institution dedicated solely to promoting peace and non-violence on a global scale.

The International Peace Court represents a paradigm shift in the pursuit of justice and accountability. Going beyond the constraints of state consent, this envisioned court would possess the authority to hold nations accountable for aggression, arbitrate disputes, and seek diplomatic solutions to prevent conflicts from escalating into war. Grounded in the collective will of the international community, this institution would symbolize humanity's unwavering commitment to forging a path toward a world free from the horrors of armed hostilities.

This creative vision of an International Peace Court encompasses more than just a judicial body; it becomes a platform for dialogue, empathy, and understanding among nations. Encouraging diplomacy and cooperation seeks to reshape the narrative of international relations, paving the way for collaborative solutions to global challenges. The court aspires to be a bastion of enlightenment, inspiring a cultural transformation where the pursuit of peace takes precedence over the pursuit of power.

However, the road to establishing the International Peace Court has obstacles. The complexities of geopolitics, entrenched rivalries among nations, and skepticism about the effectiveness of international mechanisms present formidable challenges. Yet, the urgency to prevent catastrophic conflicts and secure a sustainable global future calls for unwavering determination and bold steps toward realizing this visionary institution.

In this chapter, we embark on a journey of innovation, exploring a realm where the dreams of lasting peace are not relegated to the realm of aspiration but become tangible possibilities. As we delve deeper into this concept, we shall critically examine its potential impact on global affairs, its legal framework, and the transformative role it could play in shaping a world where the triumph of diplomacy and understanding replaces the devastation of war. The International

Peace Court beckons us to rise above the shadows of the past and step into a future where peace becomes a shared endeavor of humanity, transcending boundaries and uniting nations in the noble pursuit of a more harmonious world.

ESTABLISHING A SPECIALIZED COURT FOR PEACEFUL DISPUTE RESOLUTION

Conflicts and war have left a path of destruction, misery, and irreparable loss throughout human history. The revolutionary idea of an International Peace Court was born out of the urgent need for a radical solution to stop the repetition of such disastrous tragedies. This ground-breaking institution hopes to promote a culture of peace and non-violence worldwide by going beyond the constraints of conventional conflict resolution procedures.

At a critical juncture in history, as the world grapples with complex geopolitical dynamics and escalating conflicts, establishing an International Peace Court is imperative. The existing mechanisms for conflict resolution have proven insufficient to prevent the outbreak of armed hostilities, leading to devastating consequences for humanity. The emergence of nuclear weapons, with their unimaginable potential for destruction, is a grim reminder of the urgent need for a more effective and specialized approach to peaceful dispute resolution.

The potential impact of the International Peace Court on global affairs is profound. By transcending the barriers of sovereignty, this court would possess the authority to hold nations accountable for acts of aggression and human rights violations. Such accountability would serve as a deterrent to potential aggressors and establish a foundation for building lasting peace and reconciliation among conflicting parties. The court's impartiality and legitimacy would garner trust from nations across the globe, facilitating the resolution of disputes that have long plagued the international community.

The legal framework of the International Peace Court would pave the way for a new dimension of international law. Its creation would require comprehensive and well-defined statutes that govern its operations, jurisdiction, and enforcement mechanisms. The court would have the authority to rule on cases involving international disputes, human rights breaches, and international law infringements. It would serve as a custodian of justice, ensuring that justice, equity, and respect for human dignity guide its actions.

The International Peace Court's transformative role cannot be overstated. It would symbolize a shift from the traditional mindset that accepts war as an inevitable outcome of state disputes. By prioritizing diplomacy, dialogue, and peaceful negotiations, the court would encourage nations to seek alternative avenues for conflict resolution. This cultural shift towards non-violence would have far-reaching implications, fostering a world where disputes are settled through cooperation and compromise rather than confrontation and hostility.

Despite its promise, establishing an International Peace Court would face significant challenges. Given the complexities of geopolitical interests and long-standing rivalries, obtaining the unanimous support of all nations for such a transformative institution might prove difficult. The court's effectiveness would also rely heavily on the willingness of nations to submit to its jurisdiction and comply with its rulings. Overcoming these obstacles would necessitate a collective commitment from the international community to embrace the court as a powerful instrument for global peace.

Collaborative efforts between the court, the United Nations, and other international organizations would be paramount to harness the full potential of the International Peace Court. Partnerships with regional bodies, non-governmental organizations, and civil society groups would enhance the court's reach and impact. By working together, these entities can create a robust network of support and advocacy for peaceful dispute resolution, further strengthening the court's position as a transformative force for global peace.

The establishment of a specialized court for peaceful dispute resolution, the International Peace Court, represents a bold step towards shaping a world where the triumph of diplomacy and understanding replaces the devastation of war. With its potential impact on global affairs, robust legal framework, and transformative role in fostering a culture of peace, the court embodies humanity's unwavering commitment to preventing armed conflicts and promoting harmonious coexistence. While challenges may lie ahead, the promise of sustainable peace and the aspiration for a brighter future call for relentless efforts in realizing the vision of an International Peace Court – a symbol of hope, justice, and a world united in its pursuit of lasting peace.

JURISDICTION AND SCOPE OF THE INTERNATIONAL PEACE COURT

Amidst the complexities of international relations, the world witnesses a continuous emergence of conflicts and disputes, inflicting immense suffering and shaking the foundation of stability. To confront this urgent challenge head-on, the concept of an International Peace Court has risen, offering a glimmer of hope for a peaceful resolution and global accord. Envisioned as an unbiased and authoritative entity, the International Peace Court aspires to adjudicate matters of international conflict, fostering a culture where peace and non-violence thrive.

In the intricate web of geopolitical interactions, disputes can arise for diverse reasons, be it territorial claims, resource conflicts, or human rights violations. These conflicts, when left unresolved, possess the potential to escalate into destructive wars and lasting animosities. The idea of the International Peace Court has drawn attention as a compelling approach to address the core causes of conflicts and create a platform for peaceful interaction in recognition of the need for a framework to prevent such hazards.

The International Peace Court originates in the aftermath of both catastrophic World Wars. A comprehensive reevaluation of the tenets guiding international relations was required due to the enormous toll of military conflicts. As a result, the United Nations (UN) and the International Court of Justice (ICJ), sometimes referred to as the World Court, were established in 1945. The ICJ was established as the UN's judicial branch with the primary duty of mediating international disputes. This important development laid the groundwork for the International Peace Court, an organization dedicated to promoting peaceful coexistence and preventing the horrors of war.

The jurisdiction of the International Peace Court encompasses a broad spectrum of conflicts and disputes between nation-states. However, parties must willingly submit to the court's jurisdiction, underscoring their commitment to resolving conflicts through peaceful measures. Territorial claims, border disputes, resource conflicts, and disagreements over international treaties may all be the genesis of the issues brought before the court. Additionally, the court has the power to deal with human rights abuses nations have perpetrated against people or groups within their jurisdiction, reiterating its commitment to maintaining human dignity and defending fundamental rights.

Additionally, the court's jurisdiction includes prosecuting crimes against peace, such as aggression and similar offenses, underscoring its role in deterring acts of hostility and upholding the principles of international law.

In terms of scope, the International Peace Court employs various mechanisms to promote peaceful dispute resolution. The court actively encourages parties to engage in diplomatic settlements, emphasizing the importance of dialogue and negotiation in resolving conflicts. Furthermore, the court may engage in mediation and conciliation efforts to facilitate amicable settlements, offering an alternative approach to adversarial proceedings. Additionally, the court has the authority to provide authoritative interpretations of international law and improve legal clarity by issuing advisory opinions on legal issues presented to it by recognized UN organizations and specialized agencies.

Detailed legislation that describes the International Peace Court's jurisdiction, membership, and processes governs its operations. The UN General Assembly and Security Council pick the court's unbiased, experienced justices, assuring consistency and impartiality in its rulings.

Proceedings before the court are conducted with due process, guaranteeing equitable treatment of all parties involved. The court applies established legal standards, including principles of international law and treaties, to guide its rulings.

The potential impact of the International Peace Court on global affairs is profound and multifaceted. By providing a forum for peaceful dispute resolution, the court significantly contributes to conflict prevention and resolution, aligning perfectly with the UN's primary objective of maintaining international peace and security. Moreover, the court's authority to address human rights violations emphasizes its role in promoting accountability for state actions that violate fundamental human rights, thus reinforcing the global commitment to upholding human dignity. In this regard, the court plays a crucial role in strengthening the rule of law at the international level, as its authoritative rulings and legal opinions contribute to the development and consistent application of international law.

In the turbulent world of international relations, establishing an International Peace Court symbolizes hope and aspiration for a world where conflicts are resolved through diplomacy and mutual understanding. Its extensive jurisdiction and broad scope exemplify its commitment to promoting global harmony, and its impartiality, legal framework, and transformative potential underscore its role as an essential pillar in the quest for a harmonious and peaceful world. As nations grapple with complex challenges, the International Peace Court remains an unwavering ally in pursuing collective security and peaceful coexistence.

The transformative potential of the International Peace Court extends beyond the realm of resolving conflicts between nation-states. As part of its duties, the court must also redress breaches of human rights, promote accountability, and preserve the ideals of justice and equality. The court empowers victims and strengthens the idea that no organization—regardless of size or power—is above the law by giving individuals and organizations a forum to demand justice for human rights violations perpetrated by nations.

In this context, the International Peace Court plays a pivotal role in ensuring that perpetrators of gross human rights violations face legal consequences for their actions. This aspect contributes significantly to the global promotion and protection of human rights, reinforcing that the international community places paramount importance on safeguarding human dignity and fundamental freedoms.

Moreover, the court's jurisdiction over crimes against peace serves as a crucial deterrent against acts of aggression and military aggression between states. The court sends a clear message that aggression will not go unpunished by prosecuting those responsible for inciting armed conflicts and initiating acts of aggression. This aspect of the court's jurisdiction is closely aligned with the principles enshrined in the UN Charter, which emphasize the importance of preventing the scourge of war and promoting peaceful relations among nations.

The International Peace Court's far-reaching impact on global affairs extends to developing and enforcing international law. As an authoritative judicial body, the court's rulings and advisory opinions contribute significantly to the evolution of international law and its consistent application. The court's interpretations of international law clarify complex legal issues, guiding states and international organizations in their conduct and interactions.

In this regard, the International Peace Court plays a transformative role in shaping the international legal framework, promoting coherence, and ensuring consistency in applying legal principles. As states and entities adhere to the court's rulings, a strong precedent is set for the future, fostering a more predictable and stable international order.

Strengthening the rule of law worldwide depends on creating an International Peace Court. As an unbiased judicial institution, the court offers a forum for the amicable settlement of disagreements and conflicts, lowering the likelihood of hostility and armed aggression.

The court's commitment to upholding international law and promoting the peaceful settlement of disputes is fundamental to maintaining stability and preventing the recurrence of devastating conflicts.

The court's transformative impact on global affairs lies in its jurisdiction, scope, and trust and the legitimacy it gains from the international community. The court's impartiality, transparency, and adherence to due process are essential to building trust among states and ensuring their voluntary submission to the court's jurisdiction. This trust is critical for the court's effectiveness and authority, as it allows it to exert its influence in a manner that promotes peaceful resolution and respect for international law.

However, as with any institution, the International Peace Court faces challenges that must be navigated to fulfill its mission effectively.

One of the key challenges lies in securing universal acceptance and participation from all states. While most UN member states are signatories to the ICJ's statute, there are still some notable exceptions. Notable countries such as the United States, China, and Russia have not accepted the compulsory jurisdiction of the ICJ, which limits the court's ability to address disputes involving these major powers.

Furthermore, the court's jurisdiction relies on the voluntary submission of states to its authority. While the UN Charter encourages states to settle their disputes through peaceful means, there may be instances where parties choose to pursue alternative courses of action, such as armed conflict or other unilateral measures. In such cases, the court's ability to intervene may be limited, and its potential impact on conflict resolution may be curtailed.

Another challenge the International Peace Court faces lies in enforcing its rulings and decisions. As an international court, the ICJ does not have its enforcement mechanisms, relying instead on the cooperation of states to implement its decisions. In cases where states refuse to comply with the court's rulings, the court's effectiveness in resolving disputes may be undermined, and its authority may be called into question.

To address these challenges, the International Peace Court must continue emphasizing its impartiality and effectiveness as a neutral arbiter of international disputes. The court must also build trust and cooperation with states that have not yet fully embraced its jurisdiction, engaging in diplomatic efforts to encourage their voluntary submission to the court's authority.

Additionally, the court should explore mechanisms to enhance the enforcement of its decisions, such as cooperation with regional organizations and the UN Security Council. The court's ability to collaborate with other international entities could strengthen its impact on conflict resolution and promote peace and security.

Moreover, the court should proactively raise awareness of its role and mandate among the international community. By better understanding its functions and benefits, the court can garner greater support from states and civil society, further bolstering its legitimacy and influence.

Establishing an International Peace Court represents a significant milestone in pursuing global peace and conflict resolution. The court's jurisdiction and scope encompass many disputes, and its transformative impact on global affairs is far-reaching. By providing a platform for peaceful dispute resolution, promoting accountability for human rights violations and upholding the principles of international law, the court serves as an indispensable instrument for fostering a world where conflicts are resolved through diplomacy and understanding.

However, the court faces challenges that must be addressed to realize its potential fully. Universal acceptance and participation from all states and effective enforcement mechanisms are crucial aspects that require careful consideration. As the International Peace Court continues to evolve and adapt, it holds the promise of shaping a world where the triumph of diplomacy and peaceful resolution replaces the devastation of war. The court's commitment to impartiality, fairness, and the promotion of international law will undoubtedly play a pivotal role in the quest for a harmonious and peaceful world, making it a beacon of hope in a turbulent world.

COMPLEMENTARITY WITH EXISTING LEGAL INSTITUTIONS

The necessity for strong and unified legal institutions has grown in importance with the constantly changing nature of international relations and global affairs. This idea is crucial for bolstering the international legal system and ensuring it operates properly. This theory is based on the notion that various legal bodies and procedures must collaborate in a coordinated manner, bridging gaps and supporting one another's initiatives.

At its core, complementarity seeks to enhance the efficacy of international law and justice by ensuring no legal vacuum exists and perpetrators of serious crimes are held accountable. This comprehensive approach acknowledges the diverse nature of challenges faced in the international arena and seeks to address them collectively through a harmonious collaboration among various legal institutions.

The Principle of Complementarity in International Law

The Rome Statute, which founded the International Criminal Court (ICC) in 1998, is where the complementarity concept first appeared. The International Criminal Court (ICC) is the first permanent international tribunal established to try people for the most heinous offenses, such as genocide, war crimes, crimes against humanity, and aggression. The ICC, however, only exercises jurisdiction when national legal systems are unable or unwilling to pursue such crimes, as it functions under the complementarity principle.

This principle serves as a fundamental pillar of the ICC's functioning, recognizing the primary role of domestic legal systems in addressing criminal offenses. By prioritizing national jurisdictions, the ICC aims to encourage states to strengthen their legal capacities and ensure accountability for serious crimes at the local level. Complementarity, therefore, emphasizes the role of domestic courts as the first line of defense against impunity, while the ICC serves as a backstop to ensure justice when national courts cannot fulfill their responsibilities.

The Role of Domestic Courts

Domestic courts are crucial in promoting the rule of law and upholding human rights within their respective jurisdictions. They possess the authority to prosecute individuals for crimes committed within their territory and are often best suited to address crimes that directly impact their citizens and communities.

Moreover, domestic courts have a deeper understanding of local customs, traditions, and nuances, which can enhance the quality and legitimacy of the justice they administer. This localized approach fosters greater trust among the affected population and ensures that justice is served and perceived as fair and equitable.

However, there are instances when national legal systems face challenges in prosecuting individuals responsible for serious international crimes. These challenges may stem from a lack of resources, political interference, or insufficient legal frameworks. In such cases, the principle of complementarity comes into play, allowing the ICC to step in and exercise jurisdiction.

The Role of the International Criminal Court

As a permanent international judicial body, the ICC operates based on complementarity and aims to serve as a court of last resort. The ICC's primary responsibility is to prosecute those most responsible for grave crimes when national jurisdictions are unable or unwilling to do so.

By exercising jurisdiction over cases involving serious international crimes, the ICC plays a crucial role in deterring future offenses, ensuring accountability for perpetrators, and providing redress for victims. The ICC's status as a global institution demonstrates the international community's commitment to eradicating impunity for the most heinous crimes and advancing the ideals of justice and humanity.

The ICC's complementary approach extends beyond its role as a prosecutorial body. It also emphasizes the importance of cooperation and collaboration between the Court and national legal systems. The ICC actively engages with states to facilitate investigations and trials, recognizing that effective prosecution often requires the support and involvement of national authorities.

Complementarity in the Context of Transitional Justice

Complementarity is not limited to the relationship between the ICC and domestic courts but extends to other transitional justice mechanisms. In post-conflict and transitional societies, pursuing justice and accountability often involves a range of measures, including truth commissions, reparations programs, and traditional justice mechanisms.

These approaches can be mutually reinforcing as they address different aspects of justice and reconciliation. Truth commissions, for example, can play a vital role in uncovering the truth about past atrocities, providing a basis for accountability and healing. Reparations programs, conversely, seek to address the harm caused to victims and communities by providing compensation and support for their rehabilitation.

In this context, complementarity ensures that different transitional justice mechanisms work harmoniously to achieve comprehensive and sustainable outcomes. By complementing each other's efforts, these mechanisms can contribute to the establishment of a durable peace, as well as the prevention of future conflicts.

Complementarity with existing legal institutions represents a powerful approach to strengthening the global legal framework and ensuring the effective functioning of international justice. The principle of complementarity, as embodied in the Rome Statute, underpins the functioning of the International Criminal Court and emphasizes the primary role of domestic courts in prosecuting serious international crimes.

By promoting collaboration and cooperation between the ICC and national legal systems, complementarity seeks to ensure that accountability for grave crimes is achieved in a manner that is both fair and effective. Additionally, complementarity extends to other transitional justice mechanisms, recognizing the value of a comprehensive and coordinated approach to post-conflict societies.

FAIRNESS, IMPARTIALITY, AND TRANSPARENCY IN THE COURT'S PROCEEDINGS

A fundamental aspect of the International Peace Court's effectiveness lies in the principles of fairness, impartiality, and transparency that underpin its proceedings. The International Peace Court aims to create a just and equitable world where conflicts are resolved peacefully and diplomacy triumphs over hostility. By ensuring fairness, impartiality, and transparency in its proceedings, the court not only upholds the rule of law but also fosters an environment conducive to lasting peace.

Fairness in the Court's Proceedings

1. Equitable Access to Justice: The equitable access to justice principle is a cornerstone of the International Peace Court's commitment to fairness. This means that all parties involved in a dispute, regardless of their status or power, have an equal opportunity to present their case and defend their interests. By ensuring that each party is heard and their arguments are given due consideration, the court promotes a level playing field that enhances the legitimacy of its decisions.

2. Adherence to Due Process: Fairness in the court's proceedings is also maintained through strict adherence to due process. This includes giving the parties adequate notice, time to prepare their case, and the right to legal representation. By upholding due process, the court guarantees that decisions are based on the case's merits rather than procedural irregularities.

3. Impartiality of Judges: The selection of impartial and qualified judges is essential to maintaining fairness in the court's proceedings. Impartiality ensures that judges do not have any preconceived biases or affiliations that could compromise their ability to render unbiased decisions. The court's credibility and trustworthiness are bolstered when its judges demonstrate integrity and independence.

Impartiality in the Court's Proceedings

1. **Objective Decision-Making:**
   Impartiality is at the core of the International Peace Court's approach to conflict resolution. Its judges are in charge of objectively evaluating the facts and legal defenses the parties make without taking a side. This commitment to impartiality enhances the court's ability to make fair and reasonable rulings.

2. **Avoidance of Political Influence**
   To uphold impartiality, the court must remain insulated from political pressures or interference. It operates solely based on principles of international law and the pursuit of justice. Shielding the court from external influences ensures that its decisions are not swayed by geopolitical interests but are guided by a commitment to uphold the rule of law.

3. **Inclusion of Diverse Perspectives**
   The International Peace Court strives to ensure the inclusion of diverse perspectives in its proceedings. This may involve appointing judges from different regions and legal traditions to bring a range of insights to the table. Embracing diversity fosters a more comprehensive understanding of complex international disputes and enhances the court's impartiality.

Transparency in the Court's Proceedings

1. **Public Access to Information:** Transparency is critical to the court's proceedings. Making relevant information accessible to the public, subject to necessary safeguards enhances accountability and trust. Public access to information allows interested parties and stakeholders to follow the proceedings and understand the basis for the court's decisions.

2. **Open Hearings:** The International Peace Court seeks to conduct open hearings whenever possible to promote transparency. Open hearings allow the public to observe the presentation of evidence and legal arguments, providing insight into the court's decision-making process. However, the court may also hold closed hearings in exceptional circumstances to protect sensitive information or the safety of witnesses.

3. **Publicly Accessible Decisions:** After reaching a decision, the court issues publicly accessible judgments that outline the reasoning behind its conclusions. These judgments serve as essential documents for scholars, practitioners, and the public to understand the legal principles applied and the court's interpretation of international law.

In pursuing lasting peace and preventing war, the International Peace Court is vital in ensuring fairness, impartiality, and transparency in its proceedings. The court promotes fairness by providing equitable access to justice, upholding due process, and selecting impartial judges. The court upholds impartiality by remaining objective, avoiding political influence, and embracing diverse perspectives. And through public access to information, open hearings, and publicly accessible decisions, the court promotes transparency.

These principles are not mere formalities but the bedrock of just and peaceful world order. By embodying these values, the International Peace

Court inspires confidence, fosters trust, and encourages compliance with its decisions. The court's commitment to fairness, impartiality, and transparency is a testament to its dedication to upholding the rule of law and promoting global harmony. As conflicts continue to arise in an increasingly interconnected world, the International Peace Court stands as a powerful force for justice, accountability, and, ultimately, the prevention of war.

CHAPTER 10

PRODUCTIVE DIALOGUE FOR PEACE

In our diverse world, we encounter a myriad of differences, ranging from cultural and religious beliefs to languages and ethnicities. Often, these diversities are celebrated as a source of richness, like the array of cuisines that tantalize our taste buds. However, regrettably, certain differences are perceived as problematic, sparking conflicts that mar our societies. Across the globe, we witness various forms of violence rooted in social conflicts, where irreconcilable cultural, religious, or ethnic differences are used to justify animosity.

So, how can we rise above these differences and misunderstandings? How can we turn disagreements into chances for cooperation and development? Dialogue is key because it is a potent instrument that may close gaps, reveal unnoticed connections, and promote respect for differences.

Dialogue can potentially mend misperceptions and negative feelings, dispelling stereotypes and discrimination. By engaging in honest conversations, we can identify shared values and common ground, paving the way for peaceful coexistence. Through dialogue, we transcend divisive labels and come together as human beings, united in our quest for inclusive solutions to today's challenges.

In recognition of the transformative power of dialogue, the Dialogue for Peace invites world leaders to embrace this vital skill daily. With the aid of the activities in the Dialogue for Peace guidelines, leaders are empowered with the tools and competencies to actively participate in decision-making and conflict resolution worldwide, fostering sustainable development. Through the Dialogue for Peace, leaders can earn the Dialogue for Peace badge, a symbol of their commitment to promoting understanding and harmony.

As we embark on the journey towards productive dialogue for peace, let us unite as global citizens, bridging divides and sowing seeds of empathy and compassion. Together, through dialogue, we can create a world where peace reigns, and conflicts yield opportunities for growth and collaboration.

THE MECHANICS OF FAIR AND PRODUCTIVE DIALOGUE

In an increasingly turbulent world, where conflicts and wars persistently loom, the profound impact of fair and productive dialogue emerges as a beacon of hope. Amidst the chaos and uncertainties, communication, in its artful form, unveils itself as a mighty force capable of bridging divides, fostering empathy, and cultivating the seeds of enduring peace among nations.

The transformative potential of dialogue lies in its ability to transcend barriers and unite even the staunchest adversaries. It operates as a powerful conduit that allows diverse perspectives to converge, offering a platform for understanding and reconciliation. By embracing the principles of fairness and productivity, dialogue becomes a formidable tool that can mend deep-seated grievances and establish common ground.

In the corridors of power and on the global stage, the significance of dialogue cannot be overstated. It holds the key to breaking the shackles of hostility and forging connections based on mutual respect and trust. Through meaningful and constructive conversations, leaders can navigate complex geopolitical landscapes and envision a future where peaceful coexistence prevails over conflict.

Fair dialogue serves as the bedrock for productive communication. It centers on the principles of honesty, openness, and impartiality. In a fair dialogue, all parties are given an equal platform to express their opinions, emotions, and grievances without fear of retribution or judgment. Active listening is an essential aspect of fair dialogue, as it demonstrates genuine interest in understanding the perspectives of others.

Productive dialogue, on the other hand, goes beyond mere conversation. It seeks tangible outcomes, such as conflict resolution, consensus-building, and cooperation. To be productive, dialogue must be well-structured, focused, and goal-oriented. World leaders engaging in productive dialogue must clearly understand the issues at hand, identify common interests, and explore potential solutions collaboratively.

The Role of Fair and Productive Dialogue in Conflict Resolution

Misunderstandings, miscommunications, and divergent perceptions are at the heart of many conflicts. Fair dialogue plays a crucial role in mitigating these factors. Leaders can better comprehend the underlying factors causing the disagreement and seek to find a solution by promoting open and honest communication.

Empathy, a key component of fair dialogue, is vital for conflict resolution. World leaders must empathize with the suffering and concerns of the affected parties to understand the human cost of war. When leaders can see the conflict through the eyes of their adversaries, it becomes easier to bridge gaps and find compromises that address the core issues at stake.

Moreover, fair dialogue helps to establish trust between conflicting parties. In the absence of trust, cooperation is nearly impossible. By engaging in transparent and respectful communication, world leaders can rebuild trust and create a conducive atmosphere for peaceful negotiations.

Building Lasting Peace through Peaceful Diplomacy

To settle wars and preserve lasting peace, world leaders must approach dialogue with a mindset of reconciliation and collaboration. This involves transcending ego and embracing humility, recognizing that peace is more valuable than dominance. The following are essential steps that leaders can take to engage in peaceful dialogue effectively:

1. **Willingness to Engage:** First and foremost, world leaders must engage in dialogue without preconditions. The desire for peace should supersede all other considerations. Leaders can set a positive tone for the dialogue process by showing a genuine willingness to negotiate.

2. **Mediation and Third-Party Involvement:** In complex conflicts, impartial mediators or third-party facilitators can be instrumental in guiding the dialogue process. These neutral actors can provide fresh perspectives, identify common ground, and help keep the conversation focused and constructive.

3. **Inclusive Dialogue:** All relevant stakeholders must be included in the dialogue process to ensure lasting peace. Excluding any party can lead to lingering resentments and potential future conflicts. Inclusivity fosters a sense of ownership and responsibility for the outcomes of the dialogue, increasing the chances of a successful resolution.

4. **Communication and Understanding:** Effective communication is the bedrock of productive dialogue. World leaders must communicate

clearly and respectfully, avoiding inflammatory language or personal attacks. Active listening and a willingness to understand the perspectives of others can lead to breakthroughs in resolving complex issues.

5. **Exploring Creative Solutions:** A productive dialogue should be open to exploring innovative solutions beyond traditional approaches. Creative thinking can lead to win-win outcomes that address the interests of all parties involved.

6. **Patience and Perseverance:** Dialogue is rarely linear, and setbacks are not uncommon. World leaders must exhibit patience and perseverance, even in the face of challenges or delays. Peaceful dialogue takes time, but the rewards are worth the effort.

Fair and productive dialogue mechanics provide a pathway to settling wars and preserving lasting peace in local and international contexts. Peaceful diplomacy is not without its challenges, but the dividends of sustainable peace make it a worthy pursuit for the greater good of humanity. Through dialogue, we can build a world where conflicts are resolved without violence and lasting peace becomes a reality.

ACTIVE LISTENING AND EMPATHY-BUILDING TECHNIQUES

When conflicts and strife arise or start looming, the pursuit of lasting peace becomes an urgent and paramount goal. In these turbulent times, the transformative power of active listening and empathy-building techniques emerges as a beacon of hope. These techniques form an artful interplay of communication and understanding, possessing the profound potential to turn adversarial relationships into harmonious dialogues, paving the way for reconciliation and peaceful coexistence.

Amidst the chaos and uncertainties, active listening and empathy are powerful catalysts for positive change. They hold the key to transcending barriers of misunderstanding and animosity, fostering genuine connection and mutual respect. By delving into the mechanics and essence of these techniques, we unlock a world where conflicts are met with compassionate understanding, empathy, and a commitment to finding common ground for resolution.

The intricate dance of active listening and empathy-building set the stage for transformative conversations. It goes beyond mere communication, as it demands a profound openness to hear and comprehend the emotions and perspectives of others truly. This empathetic engagement creates safe spaces for individuals to express themselves without fear of judgment, paving the way for authentic and constructive dialogue.

The Essence of Active Listening

With its intricate artistry, active listening extends far beyond the surface of hearing, weaving a profound tapestry of meaningful communication that demands our unwavering engagement and undivided presence. When practiced in peaceful dialogue, its impact is nothing short of magical.

In this enchanting exchange, active listeners skillfully extend their full attention, engaging like graceful dancers in a symphony of understanding. The maintaining of eye contact mirrors the depths of their genuine interest, while nods, smiles, and encouraging words compose a symphony of non-verbal affirmations, a reassuring melody that tells the speaker their voice is heard and valued.

In this safe and nurturing environment, speakers find the courage to shed their inhibitions, expressing themselves authentically and honestly. The active listener becomes a trusted ally, a comforting embrace with space for vulnerability. Empathy takes center stage in this delicate dance of connection, flourishing as the listener immerses themselves in the speaker's emotions and perspectives. Bonds are formed, transcending the boundaries of difference.

The essence of active listening lies in the art of understanding beyond mere words – the ability to hear the unspoken, grasp the nuances of the heart, and acknowledge the unexpressed fears and hopes. Empathy blossoms like a resplendent flower as this profound connection unfold, fostering a profound sense of togetherness that nurtures lasting bonds. Within peaceful dialogue, active listening becomes the catalyst for a world where compassion reigns, conflicts dissolve, and lasting peace becomes an attainable reality.

Mechanics of Active Listening

At the core of active listening lies the genuine desire to comprehend the speaker's emotions, thoughts, and perspectives. Reflective listening, a fundamental aspect, involves paraphrasing or summarizing the speaker's words to confirm mutual understanding. Inclusive and non-judgmental, active listening invites vulnerability and authenticity, facilitating a more profound exchange of ideas and emotions.

Empathy as a Transformative Force

Empathy is the key to unlocking human connection, bridging divides, and nurturing understanding. As individuals cultivate empathy, they develop the capacity to step into the shoes of others, recognizing and validating their feelings and experiences. This emotional resonance forms the basis for genuine compassion and the potential for profound transformation in interpersonal relationships and broader social dynamics.

Cultivating Empathy

Empathy-building techniques encompass understanding others' perspectives and emotions, especially in conflict or disagreement.

Through active engagement and emotional intelligence, individuals can set aside personal biases, embrace cultural sensitivities, and approach dialogues with an open heart and mind. By practicing empathy, they create an inclusive and empathetic space, fostering the grounds for peaceful resolutions.

The Role of Active Listening and Empathy in Peaceful Dialogue

1. Creating Safe Spaces for Dialogue
   Active listening and empathy-building techniques cultivate an environment of trust and respect, paving the way for safe and open dialogue. Participants feel heard and valued, encouraging them to share their deepest concerns and hopes, unearthing the common ground necessary for resolution.

2. Resolving Conflicts with Empathy
   In conflicts, empathy acts as a powerful de-escalation tool. By truly understanding the emotions and perspectives of others, individuals can transcend hostility, replacing it with a shared humanity and a willingness to find common ground. Empathetic communication enables creative problem-solving, cooperation, and reconciliation.

3. Building Bridges in International Relations
   At the international level, active listening and empathy hold the potential to bridge cultural gaps and foster diplomatic relations. World leaders who embrace empathy can navigate complex geopolitical landscapes, build alliances, and prioritize peaceful resolutions over aggression.

Techniques for Enhancing Active Listening and Empathy

- Mindfulness and Presence
  Mindfulness enables individuals to be fully present in the moment, offering undivided attention to the speaker. By practicing

mindfulness, listeners can set aside distractions and immerse themselves in the dialogue, fostering a deeper understanding of the conveyed emotions and perspectives.

- Reflective Listening
  Reflective listening involves paraphrasing the speaker's words to ensure mutual understanding. This technique confirms that the listener has absorbed the message accurately and empathetically, facilitating more meaningful exchanges.

- Non-Judgmental Approach
  Avoiding judgment is essential in active listening and empathy-building. By suspending preconceived notions and biases, individuals create a safe space for honest communication and vulnerability, enhancing the potential for resolution and healing.

- Cultivating Emotional Intelligence
  Emotional intelligence allows individuals to recognize and manage their emotions while empathetically understanding others' feelings. Individuals can approach conversations with empathy and compassion by developing emotional intelligence and fostering deeper connections and understanding.

Overcoming Challenges in Active Listening and Empathy

- Cultural Sensitivity: Cross-cultural communication can present challenges in understanding diverse perspectives. By embracing cultural sensitivity and respecting differences, individuals can navigate potential misunderstandings and bridge cultural gaps.

- Managing Emotional Triggers: Active listening and empathy require emotional resilience. Listeners may encounter triggers that evoke strong reactions, potentially hindering their ability to empathize fully. Learning to manage emotional triggers enables listeners to remain open and compassionate in challenging conversations.

Active listening and empathy-building techniques form the cornerstone of peaceful dialogue and lasting peace. By embracing these transformative practices, individuals and world leaders can create safe spaces for meaningful interactions, resolve conflicts with empathy and understanding, and forge connections that transcend divisions. As we cultivate these skills, we contribute to a more harmonious world, where dialogue becomes a force for unity and understanding, fostering a future of lasting peace and compassion for all. Let us embark on this journey of active listening and empathy-building, making our world more empathetic and peaceful for generations.

OVERCOMING COMMUNICATION BARRIERS AND CULTURAL DIFFERENCES

Effective communication is the bedrock upon which human interaction thrives, facilitating understanding, cooperation, and empathy among individuals and communities. It is the art of conveying thoughts, emotions, and ideas in a manner that is clear, respectful, and conducive to mutual comprehension. When communication is successful, it creates a bridge between people, fostering connection and empathy, enabling them to navigate challenges and resolve conflicts. In ordinary times, effective communication is a powerful tool for building relationships, encouraging collaboration, and enhancing societal cohesion.

However, communication faces formidable challenges during conflict and war that hinder the path to a peaceful resolution and escalate hostilities. In these situations, communication barriers arise, creating divisions and frictions that exacerbate the existing conflicts. These barriers may take various forms and stem from cultural, emotional, informational, and power imbalances.

Cultural differences can present significant challenges to communication during conflicts. When confronted with opposing cultures, individuals may interpret gestures, symbols, and language differently, leading to misunderstandings and unintentional offense. Cultural norms, traditions, and values can color the parties' perspectives, making it challenging to find common ground for dialogue and compromise.

Emotional turmoil and psychological trauma are inevitable consequences of conflict and war. Fear, anger, and grief grip individuals and communities, causing people to become guarded, defensive, and unwilling to communicate openly. Emotional barriers can prevent the free expression of thoughts and concerns, further isolating parties and making resolution elusive.

Information control and propaganda are common tactics employed during conflicts and wars. Conflicting parties may manipulate information, censor news, and spread biased narratives to shape public opinion and garner support. Such tactics create information gaps and fuel misinformation, making it difficult for the public to discern the truth and making productive dialogue elusive.

Power imbalances often surface during conflicts, with one side holding significantly more influence, resources, or control than the other. This disparity can silence the voices of the marginalized and oppressed, preventing them from participating in meaningful dialogue. Power dynamics can also lead to one party imposing its will upon the other, generating resentment and breeding further animosity.

The heightened stakes and intensified emotions can lead to misunderstandings and misinterpretations during conflicts and wars. In times of communication, non-verbal cues like body language and facial expressions take on even greater significance. Nevertheless, cultural disparities can lead to misinterpretations of these non-verbal cues, potentially leading to unintended conflicts and misunderstandings.

Communication barriers and differences during conflict and war are complex and multifaceted. Cultural, emotional, informational, and power-related factors all contribute to the breakdown of effective communication. These barriers hinder the establishment of trust, empathy, and cooperation among conflicting parties, making the path to a peaceful resolution seem uncertain.

To effectively address these communication barriers, it is essential to cultivate an environment of open and empathetic communication. Active listening and empathy play a pivotal role in breaking down walls and establishing a foundation for understanding. By genuinely listening to the concerns, perspectives, and emotions of others, individuals can begin to bridge the gaps and find common ground.

Bridging cultural and linguistic gaps is equally crucial in overcoming communication barriers. Employing skilled interpreters and cultural mediators can facilitate accurate translations and promote cultural understanding, fostering respect and inclusivity.

Transparency and open dialogue are fundamental in dispelling misinformation and propaganda. By providing unbiased and reliable information to the public, governments, organizations, and the media can create platforms for constructive discussions, encouraging honest exchanges of ideas and perspectives.

Addressing psychological barriers requires support and understanding for individuals affected by conflict. By creating safe spaces for people to express their emotions and traumas, healing can begin, and open communication can flourish.

Establishing neutral platforms and involving third-party facilitators can help level the playing field during conflict resolution. Neutral mediators can ensure that all parties' voices are heard, enabling fair and unbiased negotiations.

Promoting non-violent communication techniques can create a respectful and cooperative environment for dialogue. By expressing feelings and needs without resorting to aggression or blame, individuals can work towards finding common ground and lasting solutions.

Acknowledging and addressing communication barriers and differences during conflict and war is crucial to fostering peaceful dialogue and resolution. Effective communication is powerful in preventing escalation, promoting understanding, and cultivating empathy. By transcending these barriers and embracing open, honest, and empathetic communication, conflicting parties can build bridges toward peace, preventing wars and laying the foundation for lasting harmony and cooperation.

SUSTAINABLE SOLUTIONS THROUGH CONSENSUS-BUILDING AND COMPROMISE

In a world filled with overt and simmering conflicts beneath the surface, the pursuit of peace becomes an urgent and paramount goal. It is an aspiration that transcends borders, cultures, and ideologies, compelling humanity to seek solutions that can forge lasting peace at the local and global levels. Achieving this grand vision requires concerted efforts and deliberate actions that embrace the power of meaningful dialogue, consensus-building, and compromise.

Consensus-building is an artful and collaborative process that aims to bridge the chasms between individuals or groups with diverse perspectives and interests. It becomes the cornerstone for resolving conflicts and erecting solutions that can withstand the test of time. Embracing inclusivity lies at the core of consensus-building, ensuring all stakeholders have a voice in decision-making. Giving value to each participant's input fosters an environment where inclusivity empowers all parties involved.

Moreover, consensus-building lays the foundation for empathy and understanding among conflicting parties. Active dialogue and open communication foster a sense of camaraderie among these entities. They gain invaluable insights into each other's concerns and aspirations as they engage in respectful conversations. This collective understanding breaks down barriers to cooperation, and thus, the path toward peace becomes clearer.

Trust, an indispensable element in any peaceful endeavor, blossoms naturally from the collaborative nature of consensus-building. As mutual respect and trust take root, stakeholders become more inclined to work together in unison. This cultivation of trust and collaboration fosters an environment where constructive dialogue flourishes. It is within this realm that sustainable solutions find their nurturing ground.

Building consensus also stimulates originality and ingenuity in problem-solving. Participants set off on a voyage of research and discovery by incorporating a variety of viewpoints and ideas.

In the realm of potential resolutions, avenues and approaches that were previously overlooked come to light. This infusion of creativity injects vitality into the process, elevating the chances of finding the most suitable and lasting solutions.

In pursuing peace, compromise emerges as the key that unlocks the doors to sustainability. It represents the willingness of conflicting parties to seek a middle ground and make concessions to meet the needs and interests of one another. In essence, compromise demands flexibility, open-mindedness, and a genuine commitment to prioritize the collective good over individual gains.

Challenging the zero-sum mindset that often perpetuates conflicts, compromise advocates for win-win outcomes. It shifts the narrative away from one side's gain at the expense of the other. Instead, it promotes resolutions where all parties benefit and finds value. In doing so, compromise harmonizes interests, fostering a sense of unity and purpose among stakeholders.

Recognizing shared goals becomes another pivotal aspect of compromise. This practice allows conflicting parties to identify the common threads that weave through their aspirations. This newfound recognition strengthens the stakeholder bond, laying a firm groundwork for cooperation. In embracing compromise, parties commit to long-term stability by addressing the underlying issues that fuel conflicts. Instead of scratching the surface, they delve deeper into the root causes perpetuating hostilities. The solutions they devise address these issues at their core, reducing the likelihood of future disputes.

Historical grievances, often deeply embedded within the fabric of conflicts, present formidable obstacles to peace. Yet, compromise provides a pathway to overcoming these long-standing rifts. Conflicting parties can transcend historical conflicts by acknowledging past injustices and finding ways to reconcile. Compromise acts as the bridge that carries them toward a future untethered by the burdens of the past.

At the local level, the significance of consensus-building and compromise in fostering peace becomes ever more evident. Engaging in inclusive dialogue becomes imperative in communities where historical, cultural, or economic issues fuel conflicts. Embracing the principles of consensus-building and compromise, communities find themselves on the path to bridging ethnic and cultural divides. They uncover shared values that form the basis for harmonious coexistence through dialogue emphasizing inclusivity and compromise.

Resource conflicts, a prevalent issue in many communities, demand solutions that transcend individual interests. By involving all stakeholders in the dialogue, communities can find sustainable resolutions that ensure equitable access to resources. Compromise, emphasizing finding a middle ground, becomes the key to unlocking the door to a shared prosperity that benefits all.

Addressing the vulnerability of youth to radicalization presents yet another challenge to local peace. By engaging young people in dialogue and considering their perspectives, communities can address the root causes of radicalization. Compromise ensures that the concerns of the youth are not only heard but integrated into the pursuit of peace.

Strengthening local governance proves vital in fostering peace within communities. Communities establish a transparent and accountable governance framework by encouraging citizen participation in decision-making processes. As communities work together to address challenges, a sense of ownership and responsibility is nurtured, driving the pursuit of sustainable peace.

On the grand stage of international relations, fostering peace becomes a collective responsibility. Nations, international organizations, and civil society all play crucial roles in pursuing global peace. Multilateral diplomacy embodies the principles of consensus-building and compromise, enabling negotiations and dialogue between multiple nations. This cooperative approach facilitates an array of solutions to address global challenges.

Conflict mediation and peacekeeping initiatives focus on bringing conflicting parties to the negotiating table. Mediators pave the way for peaceful dialogue by employing the principles of consensus-building and compromise. Sustainable solutions can emerge through these dialogues, becoming the solid foundations for lasting peace.

Environmental challenges, such as climate change, demand global cooperation on an unprecedented scale. Embracing compromise and dialogue, nations can unite to pursue collective environmental goals. In these collaborative efforts, preserving the planet for future generations takes center stage.

Nuclear disarmament and non-proliferation efforts necessitate dialogue and compromises among nuclear and non-nuclear states. Sustainable peace in a nuclear-powered world can only be achieved through mutual trust and shared commitments to global security. By fostering a culture of compromise, nations can work together towards the shared goal of a world free from nuclear war.

The pursuit of peace demands a multifaceted approach that embraces consensus-building and compromise. Through inclusivity, empathy, and creativity in dialogue, communities can find common ground and effectively address conflicts. Compromise lays the groundwork for enduring peace with its commitment to unity and shared prosperity. From the local level to the grand stage of international relations, these principles serve as potent tools to prevent war and create a world where peace flourishes. Embracing these principles invites humanity to forge a better future where dialogue and understanding triumph over hostility and conflict. Only through the concerted effort of every individual and nation can we build a world where the pursuit of peace is an ever-unfolding reality.

CHAPTER 11

A MULTILATERAL CHARTER FOR PEACE

In a situation where conflicts have long dominated the landscape, the yearning for enduring peace and global harmony resounds deeply within the hearts of individuals and nations alike. As humanity stands at the crossroads of its destiny, a profound realization dawns upon us—that the pursuit of zero tolerance for war, terrorism, and any method of bloodshed is not just a lofty ideal but an imperative for our shared future.

This standard yet compelling aspiration guides us towards a world where swords are transformed into plowshares, nations bridge differences through dialogue and diplomacy, and the sanctity of human life stands inviolable. The quest for lasting peace transcends political boundaries and cultural divides, uniting humanity under a universal banner of hope and progress.

Beyond the clamor of discord, we find common ground—an unyielding commitment to preserving the dignity of life and fostering an environment conducive to mutual understanding. The call to action extends beyond the hallowed halls of governance; it beckons each individual to contribute their part, for peace is not merely a concept but a collective responsibility.

In this pursuit, we are not naive to the complexities that lie ahead. History has taught us harsh lessons but has also illuminated the possibilities that emerge when we prioritize diplomacy over hostility and compassion over conflict. Each step towards peace, no matter how small, resonates with the potential to ripple across borders and transform our world.

This is not a solitary journey but a shared endeavor that bridges nations and transcends generations. It calls upon leaders to rise above political expediency and prioritize the welfare of their people, recognizing that prosperity is best secured in a climate of peace and stability. It implores citizens to embrace diversity and seek dialogue, for prejudices crumble and understanding flourish in the meeting of minds.

Together, we stand on the cusp of a defining moment—an opportunity to mold the future we wish to inherit. Through concerted efforts and unwavering determination, we can rewrite the narrative of our times, scribing a story of unity, compassion, and progress.

Notably, peace is not a destination but a continuous journey—a collective effort to foster a world where the pen is mightier than the sword and the power of cooperation surpasses that of conflict. Let us dare to dream, aspire to inspire, and forge an unbreakable resolve to build a future founded on the principles of zero tolerance for war, terrorism, and any method of bloodshed.

In this chapter, we explore the contours of this vision, delving into the depths of possibility and potential. Together, let us take the first step towards a more peaceful world filled with hope, harmony, and a shared commitment to a brighter tomorrow.

MULTILATERAL CHARTER FOR PEACE: THE FRAMEWORK FOR PEACEFUL COEXISTENCE

The Multilateral Charter for Peace is a visionary document that seeks to foster global harmony and security. At its heart lies a profound commitment to cooperation and collaboration among nations, underpinned by the core principle of zero tolerance for war, terrorism, and any form of bloodshed.

The charter's vision is centered on the belief that through united efforts, nations can transcend their interests and address shared challenges more effectively. It recognizes the interconnected nature of contemporary global issues, understanding that no single country can navigate the complexities of the modern world in isolation.

The principle of zero tolerance for war, terrorism, and bloodshed is a resolute call to action against violence as a means of resolving conflicts. The charter acknowledges the devastating consequences of armed conflicts on human lives, infrastructure, and societal well-being. It underscores the urgency to seek peaceful alternatives to address disputes and disagreements among nations.

Diplomacy emerges as the keystone for conflict resolution within the multilateral charter. The charter seeks to build bridges of understanding and trust through diplomatic dialogue, negotiations, and mediation. It emphasizes that genuine strength lies not in military prowess but in the ability to communicate openly and honestly.

As nations unite in their commitment to combat terrorism, violent extremism, and the proliferation of weapons of mass destruction, collective security transforms into a shared responsibility. In the context of the charter, it is acknowledged that genuine security can only be achieved when all nations actively participate in safeguarding the safety and stability of the global community. This emphasizes the imperative for collaborative efforts among countries, underscoring the need to work together to address security challenges effectively.

While promoting cooperation, the multilateral charter also respects the sovereignty and independence of each nation. It celebrates the diversity of cultures and experiences, seeking to create an inclusive global community where mutual respect prevails. The charter aims to dismantle barriers that divide nations, promoting dialogue and understanding.

Integral to the charter's vision is integrating sustainable development as a core component. Peace and development are seen as mutually reinforcing, and nations are encouraged to prioritize responsible resource management, environmental protection, and social progress.

To cultivate a lasting culture of peace, the charter places significant emphasis on education and empathy. The charter seeks to build understanding and compassion among nations by promoting global citizenship and cultural exchange. Education becomes a powerful tool to nurture critical thinking and open-mindedness, shaping a new generation of leaders committed to peace and cooperation.

The Multilateral Charter for Peace represents a transformative initiative that envisions a world united through cooperation and collaboration. By embracing zero tolerance for war, terrorism, and bloodshed, nations take a decisive step toward fostering global harmony and security. The charter calls upon all nations to work together for mutual understanding, trust, and sustainable development. As nations commit to the ideals of the multilateral charter, a brighter future emerges—a future where diplomacy and empathy triumph over conflict and violence, paving the way for a more peaceful and prosperous world for all humanity.

UPHOLDING SOVEREIGNTY: A PIVOTAL PRINCIPLE FOR HARMONIOUS INTERNATIONAL RELATIONS

Recognizing and respecting each nation's sovereignty becomes critical in the quest for harmonious international relations and peaceful cohabitation. It is the foundation for building international trust, collaboration, and understanding. By recognizing states' sovereignty and independence, the global community may foster an atmosphere in which subnational and national governments agree to zero tolerance for war, terrorism, and other forms of crime.

Recognizing and respecting sovereignty stands as a cornerstone of modern international relations. It embodies the notion that each nation possesses the inherent right to govern its internal and external affairs without external interference. This principle is enshrined in the Charter of the United Nations and is integral to the fabric of international law.

In recognizing sovereignty, nations extend mutual respect to one another, acknowledging that no single nation has the right to dictate the internal affairs of another. It lays the groundwork for cooperation and collaboration as nations seek to dialogue and find common ground to address shared challenges.

Respecting sovereignty does not imply isolation or exclusion but emphasizes the importance of sovereign equality. It encourages nations to interact as equals, understanding that diverse perspectives and experiences enrich the global discourse. Embracing this principle enables a more inclusive and just international order where nations can forge partnerships based on mutual interests and aspirations.

When Subnational and national governments commit to recognizing and respecting each other's sovereignty, they lay a solid foundation for building trust and enhancing diplomatic relations. Diplomacy, as the primary means for conflict resolution, becomes more effective in an atmosphere of respect and equality. Nations can engage in open and constructive dialogue, mitigating misunderstandings and dispelling mistrust.

Sovereign nations have the prerogative to determine their domestic policies and governance structures, provided they adhere to international law and norms. This recognition empowers nations to implement policies that promote social progress, human rights, and economic development tailored to their unique circumstances.

In promoting harmonious relations, the sovereignty principle allows nations to unite to pursue common goals. Nations can collaborate on issues of global significance, such as climate change, pandemics, and poverty, recognizing that these challenges transcend borders and demand collective action.

Moreover, recognizing sovereignty enhances the efficacy of multilateral institutions and agreements. When nations voluntarily participate in international treaties and organizations, they affirm their commitment to resolving global issues through collective efforts. This cooperation strengthens the global governance system and reinforces the rule of law.

Central to the principle of sovereignty is the respect for territorial integrity. Borders serve as the physical manifestation of a nation's sovereignty, and any attempts to violate these borders are perceived as a threat to national security. By upholding territorial integrity, nations contribute to regional stability and prevent conflicts rooted in territorial disputes.

In this context, zero tolerance for war, terrorism, and any method of bloodshed gains even greater significance. Embracing this principle becomes imperative for protecting the sovereignty of nations and ensuring their peaceful coexistence. Armed conflicts and acts of terrorism undermine the autonomy of nations and disrupt the lives of innocent civilians, impeding social progress and development.

When Subnational and national governments commit to zero tolerance for conflict, they prioritize peaceful solutions to disputes and disagreements. They pledge to exhaust diplomatic means in resolving conflicts, seeking dialogue, mediation, and arbitration as the preferred alternatives. Doing so reinforces the principle of recognizing and respecting sovereignty, as peaceful resolution preserves the dignity and autonomy of the nations involved.

Zero tolerance for war, terrorism, and any method of bloodshed transcends national boundaries. It requires nations to cooperate in combating transnational threats that endanger global security. Terrorism, being unbounded by borders, necessitates a unified response from the international community to counter its impact effectively.

Additionally, zero tolerance for conflict enhances the potential for economic development and prosperity. Nations at peace can allocate resources to social welfare, education, and infrastructure, uplifting their citizens' quality of life. Stability and security attract foreign investment and foster economic partnerships, further promoting global cooperation.

Recognizing and respecting the sovereignty of each nation stands as a fundamental principle in promoting harmonious relations and peaceful coexistence. This principle creates a framework where Subnational and national governments can agree to zero tolerance for war, terrorism, and any method of bloodshed. By acknowledging the autonomy and equality of nations, the global community can forge an environment where diplomatic dialogue thrives and peaceful conflict resolution prevails. Upholding sovereignty reinforces the rule of law and enhances the effectiveness of international cooperation. Together, with an unwavering commitment to zero tolerance for conflict, nations can pave the way for a future of global harmony, security, and shared prosperity.

COMBATING TERRORISM AND EXTREMISM

Combating terrorism and extremism has emerged as a critical worldwide concern. As these risks loom, large, subnational, and national governments acknowledge the critical necessity for collaborative efforts and unshakable collaboration across states to meet this common problem. Only by pooling their resources will they be able to mount a credible fight against these evil forces.

Terrorism and extremism have emerged as pervasive threats, transcending borders and ideologies. They feed on chaos, instilling fear and division among communities. To confront these challenges effectively, subnational and national governments must foster intelligence sharing, coordinated law enforcement, and robust counterterrorism initiatives that extend beyond individual interests.

Intelligence sharing lies at the heart of a united front against terrorism. By pooling their knowledge and resources, subnational and national governments create a comprehensive and dynamic picture of potential threats. No nation stands alone in this battle; instead, they stand shoulder to shoulder, united by a common purpose: to safeguard the safety and security of their citizens. There are no distinctions or hierarchies in intelligence sharing—only the collective pursuit of knowledge to dismantle the networks that breed terror.

Coordinated law enforcement becomes the backbone of their defense against terrorism and extremism. Borders hold no barriers when subnational and national governments coordinate their actions, ensuring that those who seek to disrupt their way of life find no refuge. Together, their unwavering commitment to upholding the rule of law becomes an indomitable force that leaves no room for terrorists to operate with impunity. This collective stand sends a compelling message: terrorism finds no sanctuary.

Yet, as they forge this united front, subnational and national governments must recognize that the roots of terrorism often stretch deep into the soil of socioeconomic disparities and ideological extremism. To address terrorism effectively, they must address its underlying causes equally.

The scourge of poverty and marginalization can leave vulnerable populations susceptible to extremist ideologies. As they combat terrorism, subnational and national governments must invest in uplifting communities and ensuring access to education, opportunities, and hope. A sense of belonging and purpose can extinguish radicalization's allure, rendering extremist ideologies' promises hollow echoes.

Ideological extremism, too, finds nourishment in the shadows of ignorance and disillusionment. It is imperative that subnational and national governments engage in open dialogue and foster a culture of tolerance and acceptance. Education becomes their most potent weapon, enlightening minds and empowering individuals to think critically and independently. They dismantle the foundations upon which extremism thrives by promoting dialogue and understanding.

At the same time, countering extremism requires an honest assessment of their societies. It is through introspection that they address grievances and create an environment where inclusivity is more than a mere aspiration—it becomes a way of life. By embracing diversity and multiculturalism, they set a precedent for a harmonious coexistence that quells the seeds of extremism.

The road ahead is undoubtedly arduous, but as subnational and national governments unite in purpose, the horizon gleams with hope. Their journey is not simply one of elimination but also a quest to build a world where the shadows of terrorism and extremism recede. It is a world defined by compassion, understanding, and justice—where all individuals are empowered to rise above hatred and violence.

In this world, they forge alliances of peace, where intelligence sharing and coordinated law enforcement are not just strategies but symbols of solidarity. They eradicate the roots of terrorism, recognizing that the battle for peace extends far beyond physical confrontations. It is a battle fought on education, opportunity, and dialogue.

So, together, subnational and national governments take the first steps towards a safer and more harmonious future. They join hands and stand as beacons of resilience, united by their shared determination to combat terrorism and extremism. As they embark on this journey, let the world witness their unwavering commitment to the values that define them: peace, compassion, and understanding.

In the unity of nations, they find the strength that will withstand the winds of extremism and the tides of terror. Their pursuit of a world free from fear is not a distant dream—it is a collective endeavor, a testament to the indomitable spirit of humanity. With courage and compassion, they will prevail, for the light of unity is more potent than the darkest shadows that threaten the world.

Together, as one global community, subnational and national governments rise against the tide of terrorism and extremism, leaving behind a legacy of peace and hope for generations to come. They forge ahead with conviction and compassion, for their unity is the most formidable force in adversity. The path may be challenging, but their resolve is unwavering. As they combat terrorism and extremism together, they pave the way toward a brighter and more secure world—a world defined by its unshakable commitment to peace and its enduring respect for the sovereignty of each nation.

HUMANITARIAN PRINCIPLES AND HUMAN RIGHTS

The unshakable devotion to humanitarian ideals and human rights shines brightly in the midst of conflict's darkest hours amid the chaos and turbulence that ruin the lives of countless individuals. In times of conflict and struggle, our collective responsibility as a global society is to defend the ideals that characterize our shared humanity. In these times, our acts transcend boundaries, transcending differences and uniting us in our search for compassion and justice.

At the core of any conflict are innocent lives caught in the crossfire—refugees fleeing the terrors of war, civilians facing the brunt of violence, and vulnerable populations struggling to survive. As we confront these harrowing realities, we must stand resolute in our conviction to protect and uphold humanitarian principles and human rights.

The importance of these principles lies not only in their moral significance but also in their practicality. Embracing humanitarian principles affirms our collective responsibility to alleviate suffering and uphold human dignity. In times of conflict, adherence to these principles becomes a beacon of hope, guiding our actions to ensure the safety and well-being of those affected.

Foremost among these principles is the imperative to protect vulnerable populations, especially refugees and civilians. As guardians of human rights, we must provide a haven for those forced to flee their homes in search of safety and solace. We must offer compassion and solidarity to civilians trapped in the crossfire, shielding them from harm and enabling access to essential services such as food, shelter, and medical aid.

Yet, mere promises are not enough; tangible safeguards must fortify our commitment. We must advocate for establishing robust mechanisms that protect and support vulnerable populations during conflict. These safeguards should encompass comprehensive strategies to address the root causes of vulnerability, ensuring those affected are not left defenseless in the face of adversity.

Establishing international mechanisms to monitor and address violations during conflicts is central to protecting humanitarian principles and human rights. Such mechanisms serve as a powerful deterrent against human rights abuses, holding perpetrators accountable for their actions. By promoting transparency and accountability, we pave the way for justice to prevail, even amidst the chaos of war.

In times of conflict, the international community must unite in condemning human rights violations and collective action to alleviate the suffering of affected populations. By fostering collaboration and cooperation, we create a fortified front against impunity, ensuring no one is above the law.

Furthermore, we must recognize that safeguarding human rights is not just the responsibility of individual nations but a collective duty that transcends borders. Advocating for the rights of the vulnerable and voiceless is our shared responsibility, standing in solidarity with them to ensure their voices are heard and protected.

Civil society, humanitarian organizations, and all global citizens play an instrumental role in this endeavor. The strength of our response lies in our unity—a tapestry woven together by compassion, empathy, and respect for the sanctity of human life.

As we navigate the turbulent waters of conflict, let us hold fast to the beacon of humanitarian principles and human rights. Let our shared humanity and our actions guide us speak louder than words. Together, we can bring light to the darkest corners of conflict, offering hope, dignity, and protection to those who have suffered the most.

Our commitment to these principles will define our legacy in the face of adversity. Let future generations look at our actions with pride, knowing we stood as guardians of compassion and justice in the darkest times.

As we forge ahead, may we remain steadfast in our dedication to upholding humanitarian principles and human rights. Let us build a world where conflicts are resolved through dialogue, the vulnerable are shielded from harm, and the dignity of every human being is respected and protected.

Together, let us create a future where the tapestry of our shared humanity is woven with threads of compassion, justice, and hope, offering solace to those in need and transforming the world into a place of peace and solidarity.

CONCLUSION

In the quest for a world where peace triumphs over war and violence, it is paramount to recognize the dire consequences of war, locally and globally. The haunting socio-economic impacts, loss of lives, torn families, and shattered communities all bear witness to the devastating toll war inflicts on humanity. To avoid such catastrophic outcomes, the imperative lies in embracing productive dialogue for peace, consensus-building, and compromise and other potent means like Peace Accords and the impactful role of Courts in conflict resolution.

The socio-economic consequences of war reverberate far beyond the battlefields. Lives are lost, leaving behind grieving families and broken communities. The economic devastation is equally dire, as resources that could have fostered development and progress are diverted toward destruction. Poverty and instability deepen, undermining the foundation of societies. Additionally, environmental degradation, mass displacements, and strained international relations compound the fallout of war, perpetuating a cycle of suffering and animosity.

To avert such catastrophic outcomes, productive dialogue, consensus-building, and compromise offer a transformative approach to conflict resolution. Engaging all stakeholders in meaningful conversations fosters inclusivity and empathy, essential components of any sustainable peace process. Open communication nurtures understanding, building bridges of cooperation that transcend divides. Trust flourishes as conflicting parties seek creative problem-solving, realizing the power of collaboration.

Equally vital is the embrace of Peace Accords to prevent war and foster lasting peace. These formal agreements serve as binding commitments between conflicting parties, outlining terms for resolution and cooperation. Peace Accords provide a structured framework for implementing sustainable solutions, leading to reconciliation and harmony. Through such accords, former adversaries can work towards common goals, finding common ground even amidst the most entrenched conflicts.

Additionally, courts are important in resolving disputes because they provide a nonviolent option to violent confrontations. A peaceful and legal resolution of conflicts can be achieved via international courts.

By holding those responsible for crimes against humanity and atrocities accountable, these courts deter further wars.

The significance of these principles and mechanisms extends from the local level to the global stage. Armed with productive dialogue, consensus-building, and compromise, communities find paths to peace, bridging cultural divides and resolving resource conflicts. Strengthening local governance and promoting citizen participation empowers communities to take charge of their destiny, safeguarding their future from the ravages of war.

The collective efforts of nations, international organizations, and civil society become paramount on the international stage. Multilateral diplomacy, conflict mediation, climate change diplomacy, and nuclear non-proliferation are vital tools for achieving constructive resolutions. By fostering international cooperation and understanding, nations unite against global challenges, creating a safer and more prosperous world.

The journey towards lasting peace is a shared responsibility that necessitates multifaceted approaches. By embracing productive dialogue, consensus-building, compromise, Peace Accords, and Courts, we can prevent conflicts from escalating into devastating wars. Together, we can forge a world where peaceful dialogue prevails, replacing animosity and hostility with cooperation and understanding.

As we unite to pursue peace, we leave a legacy of harmony and compassion for generations. The age-old dream of a world without war can become an enduring reality through collective dedication and commitment. It is within our grasp to build a future where cooperation, empathy, and reconciliation triumph over violence and conflict. By harnessing the strength of these strategies and mechanisms, we pave the way for a world where peace becomes a universal truth. Let us stand together and sow the seeds of peace, cultivating a world where the pursuit of harmony becomes our shared endeavor.

REFERENCES

- ACCORD. (March, 2019). *Traditional methods of conflict resolution - ACCORD.*
- Staff, P. (n.d.). *Conflict resolution*. PON - Program on Negotiation at Harvard Law School.
- Team, A. O. B. (2022). 4 Signs Conflict Resolution is in Your Blood. *Abilene Christian University.*
- Murthy, R. S. (February, 2006). *Mental health consequences of war: a brief review of research findings*. PubMed Central (PMC).
- Unhcr, B. (February, 2023). Worldwide displacement hits all-time high as war and persecution increase.
- Serafino, Nina M., Peacekeeping and Related Stability Operations, New York, Novinka Books, 2005.
- Publisher, A. R. a. R. O. O. (March, 2016). *16.4 Preventing war and stopping terrorism.*
- Levy, B. S. (2022). Preventing war and promoting peace. In *Oxford University Press eBooks.*
- *Avoiding traps and preventing war: History, technology, and fear | Brookings*. (December, 2022,).
- Norberg, Annika H., "Challenges of Peace Operations", International Peacekeeping, Vol. 10,2003.
- Sullivan, P. L., & Karreth, J. (2019). Strategies and Tactics in Armed Conflict: How governments and foreign interveners respond to insurgent threats. *Journal of Conflict Resolution.*

- Micciche, J. P. (2021). THE ART OF NON-WAR: SUN TZU AND GREAT POWER COMPETITION.
- Shonk, K. (2023). 3 Negotiation strategies for conflict resolution. *PON - Program on Negotiation at Harvard Law School.*
- Public Diplomacy: A Tool for Peace and Understanding | The American Society of Administrative Professionals. (2023). *ASAP.*
- Kelman, Herbert C, "Interactive Problem Solving", Vamik V olkan et a1. (eds.), The Psychodynamics of International Relationships, London, Lexington Books, 1991.
- Ziegler, P. (May, 2023). Types Of Diplomacy And Diplomatic Practice In 21st Century. *Best Diplomats | Diplomatic Conferences | New York.*
- Serafino, Nina M., Peacekeeping and Related Stability Operations, New York, Novinka Books, 2005.
- Taylor, Rupert, Creating A Better World: Interpreting Global Civil Society, Bloomfield, CT, Kumarian Press, 2004.
- United Nations, The Blue Helmets: A Review of United Nations Peacekeeping, New York, Department of Public Information, 1990.
- Zartman, I. William and Saadia Touval, "International Mediation in the Post-Cold War Era", Chester A. Crocker et a1. (eds.), Managing Global Chaos, Washington D.C, United States Institute of Peace Press, 1996.
- Zartman, I. William and Spector I. Bertram, Getting It Done: Post-Agreement Negotiation and International Regimes, Washington, D.C, United States Institute of Peace Press, 2003.
- Pruitt, Dean G., Sung H. Kim and Jeffrey Z. Rubin, Social Conflict: Escalation and Settlement, New York, McGraw-Hill, 2004.
- Frédéric Mégret, *The Limits of the Laws of War.* In: *The Limits of Human Rights.* Edited by: Bardo Fassbender and Knut Traisbach, Oxford University Press 2019.
- Azou-Passonda, M., Wang, H., Mobogaina, Z., Kossingou, G. G., & Baoro, S. K. G. S. (2019). The failure of peace processes: the specific case of the Central African Republic. *Open Journal of Political Science.*

- UNESCO. (January, 2013). *Promoting peace, ethics, and dialogue.* UNESCO.
- Sarat, A., & Grossman, J. B. (1975). Courts and Conflict Resolution: Problems in the mobilization of adjudication. *American Political Science Review.*
- Pips. (June, 2023). Charter of Peace. *Pak Institute For Peace Studies Pvt Ltd. (PIPS).*
- Chinkin, C., & Kaldor, M. (2017). Sovereignty and the authority to use force. In *Cambridge University Press eBooks.*

ABOUT THE AUTHOR

Dr. Dominion V. Judah is a distinguished economist, visionary scientist, accomplished researcher, and prolific innovator. With an unwavering commitment to elevating lives, businesses, communities, and nations, he stands as a grand trailblazer and pathfinder in different fields, the academia and practical applications. Driven by an unyielding passion for progress, he has authored numerous bestselling books, each a testament to his relentless pursuit of knowledge and improvement, some of which include "Sub-national Prosperity," "Peace And Not War," "Economic Renaissance," "Ending Poverty", "Economics and Finance Win-Win Growth Strategies"

Dr. Dominion V. Judah epitomizes the convergence of intellectual rigor and humanitarian fervor. His profound contributions have not only enriched scholarly discourse but have also ignited tangible change in the lives of countless individuals, communities and nations. Through his visionary work, he continues to illuminate the path towards a future marked by empowered economies, poverty-free societies, world peace and lasting global transformation.

Published By: THE AGELESS PRESS
contact@theagelesspress.com

Made in the USA
Las Vegas, NV
15 November 2026

f397f096-9578-4baa-8982-9483e75733bfR01